BASEBALL CARD BOOKS
are published by

PRICE STERN SLOAN

There is a  BASEBALL CARD BOOK for every major league team. Collect them all or concentrate on your favorites.

Available for all 26 teams!

 BASEBALL CARD BOOKS are available wherever books or baseball cards are sold, or may be ordered directly from the publisher. Simply send your check or money order for $9.95 plus $2.00 for shipping and handling to—

PRICE STERN SLOAN
Cash Sales
360 North La Cienega Boulevard
Los Angeles, CA 90048

You'll find books for all 26 major league teams at the  BOOKS HEADQUARTERS STORE. To locate the HEADQUARTERS nearest you, simply call:

PRICE STERN SLOAN
(800) 421-0892
Calling from CA (800) 227-8801

BASEBALL CARDS

Text by
Larry Schwartz

PRICE STERN SLOAN
Los Angeles

Copyright © 1989 by Topps Chewing Gum, Inc.
Text and statistics Copyright © 1989 by MBKA, Inc.

Published by Price Stern Sloan, Inc.
360 North La Cienega Boulevard, Los Angeles, California 90048

ISBN 0-8431-2455-5

All rights reserved. No part of this publication may be reproduced, stored in a retrieval system, or transmitted, in any form or by any means, electronic, mechanical, photocopying, recording, or otherwise, without prior written permission of the publishers.

Officially licensed by Major League Baseball

Official Licensee

© 1988 MLBPA
© MSA

An MBKA Production

Printed and bound in Hong Kong.

TEAM LEADERS

Year-by-Year Batting Leaders

Home Runs
1962 - Roman Mejias (24)
1963 - John Bateman (10)
1964 - Walt Bond (20)
1965 - Jim Wynn (22)
1966 - Jim Wynn (18)
1967 - Jim Wynn (37)
1968 - Jim Wynn (26)
1969 - Jim Wynn (33)
1970 - Jim Wynn (27)
1971 - Joe Morgan (13)
1972 - Lee May (29)
1973 - Lee May (28)
1974 - Cesar Cedeno (26)
1975 - Cliff Johnson (20)
1976 - Cesar Cedeno (18)
1977 - Bob Watson (22)
1978 - Bob Watson (14)
1979 - Jose Cruz (9)
1980 - Terry Puhl (13)
1981 - Jose Cruz (13)
1982 - Phil Garner (13)
1983 - Dickie Thon (20)
1984 - Jose Cruz (12)
1985 - Glenn Davis (20)
1986 - Glenn Davis (31)
1987 - Glenn Davis (27)
1988 - Glenn Davis (30)

Runs Batted In
Roman Mejias (76)
John Bateman (59)
Walt Bond (85)
Jim Wynn (73)
John Bateman (70)
Jim Wynn (107)
Rusty Staub (72)
Denis Menke (90)
Denis Menke (92)
Cesar Cedeno (81)
Lee May (98)
Lee May (105)
Cesar Cedeno (102)
Bob Watson (85)
Bob Watson (102)
Bob Watson (110)
Jose Cruz (83)
Jose Cruz (72)
Jose Cruz (91)
Jose Cruz (13)
Phil Garner (83)
Jose Cruz (92)
Jose Cruz (95)
Jose Cruz (79)
Glenn Davis (101)
Glenn Davis (93)
Glenn Davis (99)

Batting Average
Roman Mejias (.286)
Al Spangler (.281)
Bob Aspromonte (.280)
Jim Wynn (.275)
Sonny Jackson (.292)
Rusty Staub (.333)
Rusty Staub (.291)
Denis Menke (.269)
Denis Menke (.304)
Cesar Cedeno (.264)
Cesar Cedeno (.320)
Cesar Cedeno (.320)
Greg Gross (.314)
Bob Watson (.324)
Bob Watson (.313)
Jose Cruz (.299)
Jose Cruz (.315)
Jose Cruz (.289)
Cesar Cedeno (.309)
Art Howe (.296)
Ray Knight (.294)
Jose Cruz (.318)
Jose Cruz (.312)
Jose Cruz (.300)
Kevin Bass (.311)
Billy Hatcher (.296)
Rafael Ramirez (.276)

Wins

- 1962 - Bob Bruce, Dick Farrell (10)
- 1963 - Dick Farrell (14)
- 1964 - Bob Bruce (15)
- 1965 - Dick Farrell (11)
- 1966 - Dave Giusti (15)
- 1967 - Mike Cuellar (16)
- 1968 - Don Wilson (13)
- 1969 - Larry Dierker (20)
- 1970 - Larry Dierker (16)
- 1971 - Don Wilson (16)
- 1972 - Larry Dierker, Don Wilson (15)
- 1973 - Dave Roberts (17)
- 1974 - Tom Griffin (14)
- 1975 - Larry Dierker (14)
- 1976 - J.R. Richard (20)
- 1977 - J.R. Richard (18)
- 1978 - J.R. Richard (18)
- 1979 - Joe Niekro (21)
- 1980 - Joe Niekro (20)
- 1981 - Nolan Ryan, Don Sutton (11)
- 1982 - Joe Niekro (17)
- 1983 - Joe Niekro (15)
- 1984 - Joe Niekro (16)
- 1985 - Mike Scott (18)
- 1986 - Mike Scott (18)
- 1987 - Mike Scott (16)
- 1988 - Bob Knepper and Mike Scott (14)

No-Hitters

- 5-17-63 Don Nottebart (vs. Phillies)
- 4-23-64 Ken Johnson (vs. Reds)
- 6-18-67 Don Wilson (vs. Braves)
- 5-01-69 Don Wilson (at Cincinnati)
- 7-09-76 Larry Dierker (vs. Expos)
- 4-07-79 Ken Forsch (vs. Braves)
- 9-26-81 Nolan Ryan (vs. Dodgers)
- 9-25-86 Mike Scott (vs. Giants)

Year-by-Year Pitching Leaders

Innings

- Dick Farrell (241.2)
- Ken Johnson (223.2)
- Ken Johnson (218)
- Bob Bruce (229.2)
- Mike Cuellar (227.1)
- Mike Cuellar (246)
- Dave Giusti (251)
- Larry Dierker (305)
- Larry Dierker (270)
- Don Wilson (268)
- Don Wilson (228.1)
- Jerry Reuss (279)
- Larry Dierker (223.1)
- Larry Dierker (232)
- J.R. Richard (291)
- J.R. Richard (267)
- J.R. Richard (275.1)
- J.R. Richard (292.1)
- Joe Niekro (256)
- Joe Niekro (166)
- Joe Niekro (270)
- Joe Niekro (263.2)
- Joe Niekro (248.1)
- Bob Knepper (241)
- Mike Scott (275.1)
- Mike Scott (247.2)
- Nolan Ryan (220)

Earned Run Average

- Dick Farrell (3.01)
- Ken Johnson (2.65)
- Bob Bruce (2.76)
- Dick Farrell (3.50)
- Mike Cuellar (2.22)
- Don Wilson (2.79)
- Mike Cuellar (2.74)
- Larry Dierker (2.33)
- Larry Dierker (3.87)
- Don Wilson (2.45)
- Don Wilson (2.68)
- Dave Roberts (2.86)
- Larry Dierker (2.89)
- Larry Dierker (4.00)
- J.R. Richard (2.75)
- J.R. Richard (2.97)
- J.R. Richard (3.11)
- J.R. Richard (2.71)
- Ken Forsch (3.20)
- Nolan Ryan (1.69)
- Joe Niekro (2.47)
- Nolan Ryan (2.98)
- Nolan Ryan (3.04)
- Mike Scott (3.29)
- Mike Scott (2.22)
- Nolan Ryan (2.76)
- Mike Scott (2.92)

April 10, 1962 Opening Day Starting Lineup

- 3B - Bob Aspromonte
- CF - Al Spangler
- RF - Roman Mejias
- 1B - Norm Larker
- LF - Jim Pendleton
- C - Hal Smith
- 2B - Joe Amalfitano
- SS - Don Buddin
- P - Bobby Shantz

Compiled by Bill Haber.

1962

The Houston Colt .45s and the New York Mets joined the N.L. as expansion teams. The Colt .45s spent more than $8 million before the season, including $3.5 million for players ($1.85 million in a draft of the unwanted of other N.L. teams). Shortstop Eddie Bressoud was the first player taken, at a cost of $75,000, by GM Paul Richards, but Bressoud was soon traded to Boston for shortstop Don Buddin. The principal owners—Bob Smith and Judge Roy Hofheinz owned more than 90 percent by December 1962—had Colt Stadium (32,601 seating capacity) built as a temporary home. Manager Harry Craft, using untried youngsters and over-the-hill veterans, led his team to a surprisingly successful season. They finished eighth at 64-96, 36½ games behind the Giants but six games ahead of the Cubs and 24 ahead of the last-place Mets. The Colt .45s won the opener 11-2 over the Cubs on April 10 behind pitcher Bobby Shantz and a pair of three-run homers by rightfielder Roman Mejias. Mejias won Houston's triple crown (.286, 24 homers, 76 RBIs) and after the season was traded to Boston for two-time A.L. batting champ Pete Runnels, who would be a bust (.253 and .196) with Houston. Bob Bruce (10-9) and Dick Farrell (10-20) were the top pitchers.

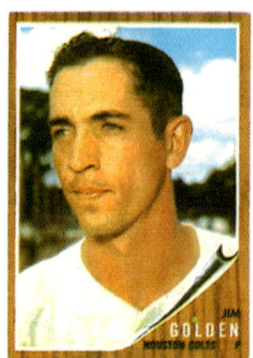

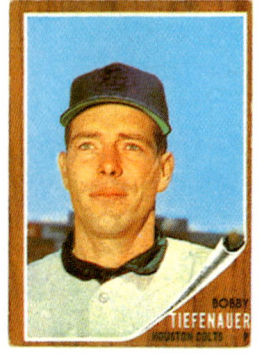

1963

Hitting was the youthful Colt .45s' problem. All they did was fire blanks. Their team batting was .220 (only the Mets' .219 was lower in the majors) and their 62 home runs were 33 fewer than any other team. In one seven-game stretch they were shut out six times. Leftfielder Al Spangler (.281) was the only regular to bat higher than .255, while 21-year-old catcher John Bateman led the team with 10 homers and 59 RBIs. Fortunately for Houston, its pitching was much better with starters Dick Farrell (14-13, 3.03 ERA), Don Nottebart (11-8, 3.17) and Ken Johnson (11-17, 2.65) and reliever Hal Woodeschick (11-0, 1.97, 10 saves). Nottebart became the first Houston player to pitch a no-hitter when he beat the Phils 4-1. The Colt .45s were amazingly successful at home (44-37), but less so on the road (22-59). Their 66-96 record left them in ninth place, 33 games behind the Dodgers but still 15 ahead of the Mets.

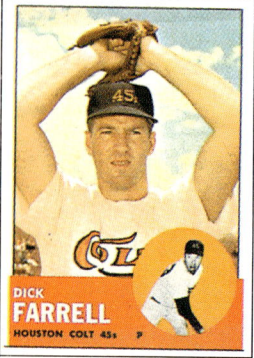

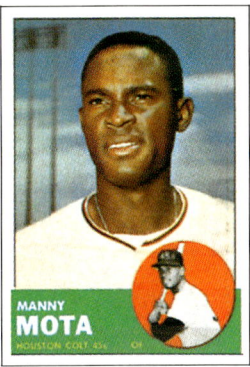

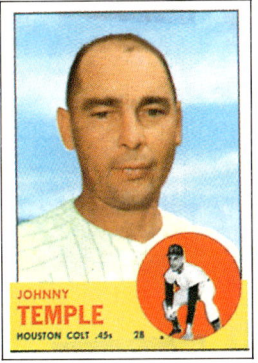

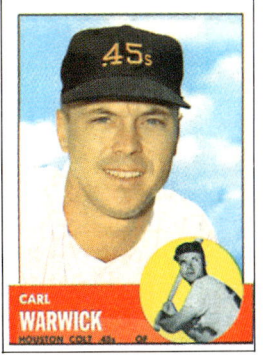

1964

Ken Johnson lost 16 games for the Colts, but none was more unusual than on April 23 when he became the first major leaguer in history to lose to a team held hitless the entire game. The Reds beat him 1-0 when Johnson made a two-base throwing error on Pete Rose's one-out bunt in the ninth inning, a groundout moved Rose to third and then he scored on an error by second baseman Nellie Fox. Dick Farrell started out blazing, being 10-1 on June 14, but won only one of his final 10 decisions to finish 11-10. Bob Bruce was the team's big winner at 15-9 with a 2.76 ERA. Third baseman Bob Aspromonte raised his average from .214 in 1963 to a team-leading .280. First baseman-outfielder Walter Bond led the team with 20 homers and 85 RBIs. Harry Craft was fired as manager on Sept. 19 with coach Luman Harris replacing him. The ninth-place Colt .45s finished 66-96 again, 27 games behind the Cards.

1965

The team changed its nickname to Astros as they moved into the "eighth wonder of the world," the Astrodome. The first domed stadium—it had air-conditioning and its roof was 208 feet high at the center—was built at a cost of $31.6 million and could seat 44,500 for baseball. The Astros drew 2,151,470 fans (almost three times as many as they did in 1964 when they attracted 725,773). But the new stadium and outpouring of fans couldn't help the Astros in the standings, where they finished ninth again, at 65-97, 32 games behind the Dodgers. Centerfielder Jimmy Wynn won the Astros' triple crown (.275, 22 homers, 73 RBIs). Joe Morgan, a rookie second baseman, showed potential, hitting .271, including a six-for-six game, scoring 100 runs, stealing 20 bases, and leading the majors by drawing 97 walks. Dick Farrell (11-11) was the only pitcher to win more than nine games. Veteran Robin Roberts, a free agent signed on Aug. 6, won his first four decisions, the first two by shutout, and finished 5-2 with a 1.89 ERA.

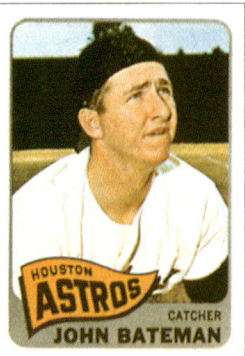

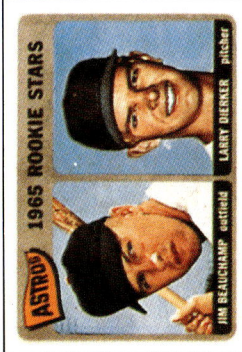

1966

Judge Roy Hofheinz, who had bought most of Bob Smith's shares to become the majority owner, fired GM Paul Richards, farm director Eddie Robinson and manager Luman Harris on Dec. 12, 1965. He made his personal assistant, Tal Smith, director of player personnel and named Grady Hatton manager. Under the new regime, the Astros started 20-12 and, for a lot of May, were in the heady atmosphere of second place. However, a 6-28 stretch in the second half, including a 1-15 streak, brought them back to earth. Still, they cracked the 70-win barrier for the first time, posting a 72-90 record, and finished in eighth place, 23 games behind the Dodgers. The Astros were now playing on synthetic AstroTurf as they learned that natural grass died under the dome. Lefthander Mike Cuellar, the ace of the staff, went 12-10 and set a still-standing team record with his 2.22 ERA, which was second in the league to Sandy Koufax's 1.73. Rookie shortstop Sonny Jackson led the team with a .292 average, 49 steals and 80 runs. Jimmy Wynn hit a team-leading 18 homers even though he missed the last two months after crashing into a wall.

BOB ASPROMONTE 3rd base

JOHN BATEMAN catcher

WALT BOND of-1st base

RON BRAND catcher

BOB BRUCE pitcher

DAN COOMBS pitcher

MIKE CUELLAR pitcher

LARRY DIERKER pitcher

 TURK FARRELL pitcher
 JOE GAINES outfield
 JIM GENTILE 1st base
 DAVE GIUSTI pitcher
 LUM HARRIS manager
 GRADY HATTON mgr.
 GARY KROLL pitcher
 BARRY LATMAN pitcher
 FELIX MANTILLA 2b-of
 LEE MAYE outfield
 JOE MORGAN 2nd base
 DAVE NICHOLSON outfield
 DON NOTTEBART pitcher
 JIM OWENS pitcher
 CLAUDE RAYMOND pitcher
 ROBIN ROBERTS pitcher

1967

The Astros used 22 pitchers as they compiled the worst ERA in the majors at 4.03. However, in this rubble were two gems—Mike Cuellar and Don Wilson. Cuellar led the team with a 16-11 record and had a 3.04 ERA. Wilson, a 22-year-old rookie righthander, went 10-9 with a team-leading 2.79 ERA. Among his victories was a no-hitter of the Braves in which he struck out 15 batters, including Hank Aaron three times. Judge Roy Hofheinz gave Wilson a $1,000 raise after the no-hitter. Three team batting records which still stand were set as Jimmy Wynn, nicknamed "The Toy Cannon," struck for 37 homers and rightfielder Rusty Staub hit .333 with a major league-leading 44 doubles. This was the first time any Houston regular ever hit .300. But Wynn and Staub had little support and the Astros went 69-93, finishing in ninth place, 32½ games behind the Cardinals.

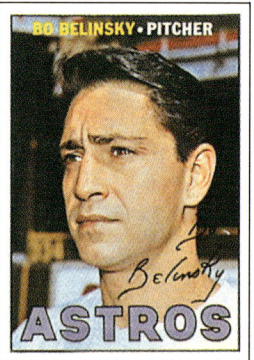

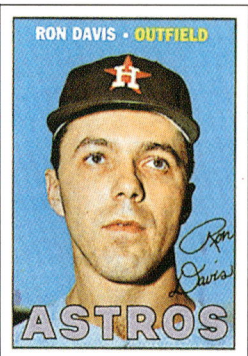

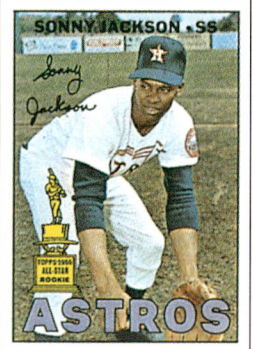
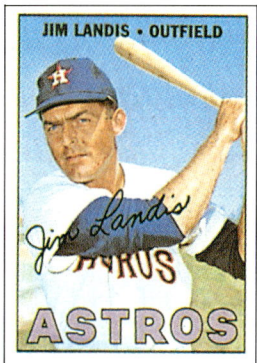
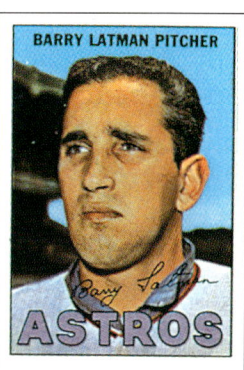

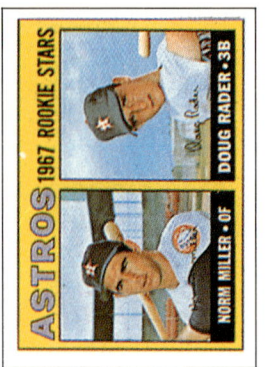

1968

Joe Morgan suffered torn knee ligaments in April and played in only 10 games. Mike Cuellar had shoulder problems and he slumped to 8-11, though he had a 2.74 ERA. Grady Hatton's pride was injured as he was fired. The Astros were 23-38 under him and 49-52 under Harry "The Hat" Walker, who had been Houston's special batting instructor. For the first time, the Astros finished last, 25 games behind the Cardinals, though their 72-90 record was an improvement over 1967. This also was the first time the Astros finished behind the Mets. The Astros did beat the Mets in the longest game of the season, 1-0 in 24 innings. Don Wilson tied the then-major league record of 18 strikeouts in a 6-1 win over the Reds. Wilson was the top winner at 13-16 while Larry Dierker (12-15), David Giusti (11-14) and Denny Lemaster (10-15) also finished in double figures. Jimmy Wynn led the team with 26 homers and tied with the Reds' Pete Rose for most assists (20) among N.L. outfielders. Rusty Staub paced the Astros with a .291 average and 72 RBIs. After the season the Astros traded Cuellar to Baltimore, Staub to Montreal, Bob Aspromonte to Atlanta and Giusti to St. Louis.

1969

The Astros had an April to forget, going 4-20 (they had losing streaks of five, seven and eight), with the month ending when Cincinnati's Jim Maloney no-hit them. But the Astros turned the season around starting the next night when Don Wilson no-hit the Reds. The Astros went 71-45 from then until Sept. 10, when they were just two games out of first place. But then came a six-game losing streak on the way to a 6-16 finish and the Astros wound up in fifth in the N.L. West (expansion teams in Montreal and San Diego caused the league to split into two six-team divisions). They were 12 games behind the Braves in their first non-losing season (81-81). They were 10-2 against the world champion Mets. Jimmy Wynn and shortstop Denis Menke became the first pair of National Leaguers ever to hit grand slams in the same inning, embarrassing the Mets with this feat. Wynn hit 33 homers and tied Eddie Stanky's N.L. record with 148 walks. Larry Dierker (20-13) became Houston's first 20-game winner and set a team record with 20 complete games. Fred Gladding had a league-leading 29 saves, a club record that would last until 1986.

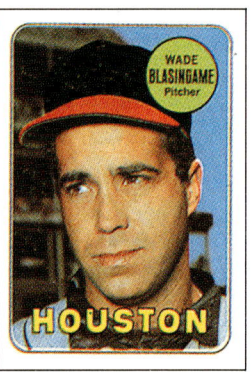
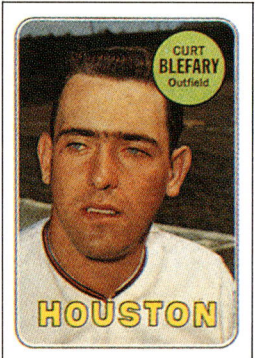

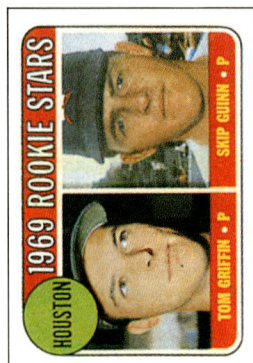

1970

The Astros made two significant changes in late June and the moves paid off handsomely. Cesar Cedeno was recalled from the minors and made the centerfielder, with Jimmy Wynn moving to left. Bob Watson became the regular first baseman. They helped the Astros to a 42-32 record after the All-Star Game as Houston moved up to fourth at 79-83, 23 games behind the Reds. Cedeno (.310), rightfielder Jesus Alou (.306) and Menke (.304, career-high 92 RBIs) all batted .300. Doug Rader hit 25 homers with 87 RBIs and won the first of five consecutive Gold Gloves at third base. Joe Morgan hit .268 with a team-leading 42 steals and 102 runs. Wynn hit 27 homers with 88 RBIs and Watson had 61 RBIs in 327 at-bats. Larry Dierker (16-12, 17 complete games), Jack Billingham (13-9) and Don Wilson (11-6) were the top pitchers. Tom Griffin, an 11-10 success as a rookie in 1969, went 3-13 and was sent back to the minors in August.

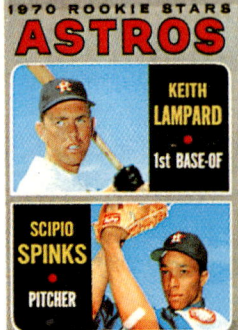

1971

The Astros were involved in an incredible 75 one-run games. Unfortunately for them, they lost 43. They finished 79-83 again and tied for fourth but this time only 11 games out, with the Giants coming in first. Disappointing seasons were had by Jimmy Wynn (.203, seven homers, 45 RBIs); and Doug Rader (12 homers, 56 RBIs). Joe Morgan's star continued rising as he led the team with 13 homers, 87 runs and 40 steals. Cesar Cedeno led the N.L. with 40 doubles and Houston with 81 RBIs. The Astros' pitching was much better than their hitting as their 3.13 team ERA was second in the N.L. to the Mets' 2.99. Don Wilson went 10-4 after the All-Star break to finish 16-10 with a 2.45 ERA. Larry Dierker (2.72 ERA) had the opposite season, gaining 12 victories by the All-Star break, but not winning another as a sore elbow limited him to only four more starts. Jack Billingham (3.39 ERA) went 10-16, losing six games 2-1.

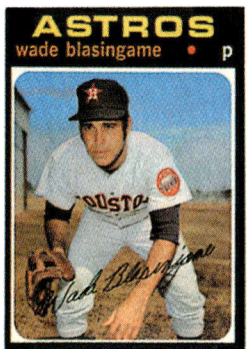

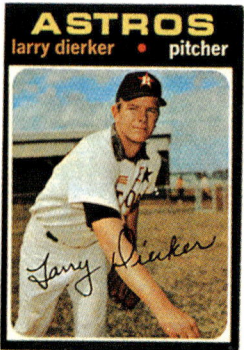

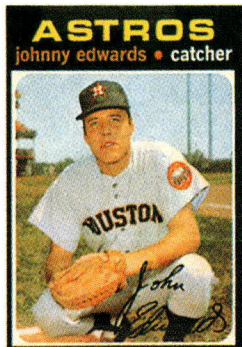
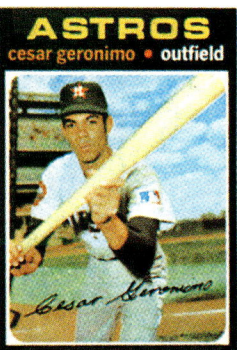

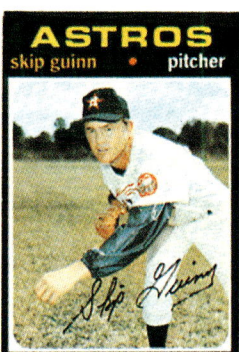
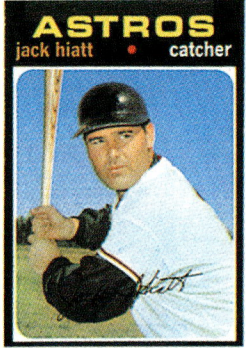

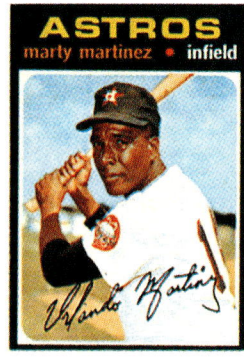

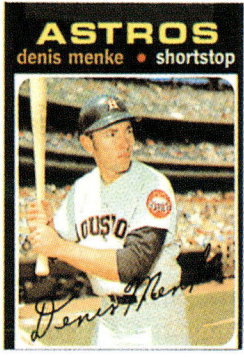
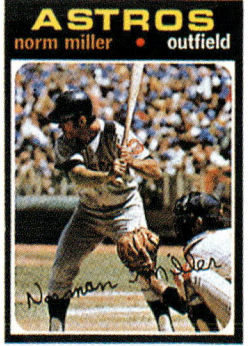

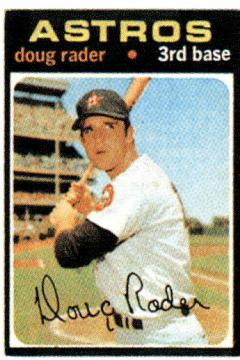

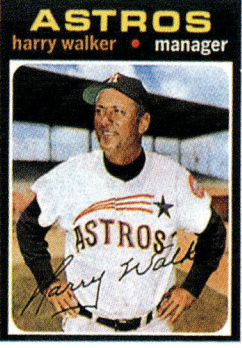

  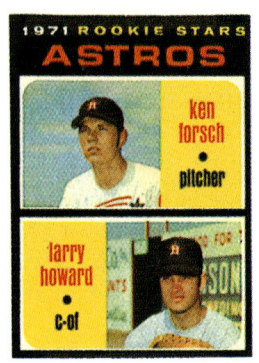 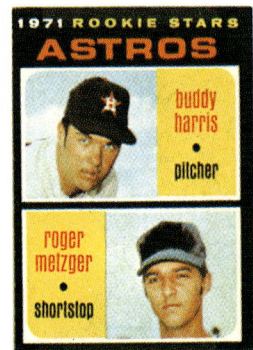

1972

The Astros made a major trade in the offseason which would benefit them in the short run. They traded future two-time MVP Joe Morgan, Denis Menke, Jack Billingham, Cesar Geronimo and Ed Armbrister to the Reds for Lee May, Tommy Helms and Jimmy Stewart. First baseman May and second baseman Helms helped the Astros to their first winning season ever. They went 84-69 to finish second, 10½ games behind the Reds in this strike-shortened season. The Astros had five players with more than 80 RBIs (May 98, Jimmy Wynn 90, Doug Rader 90, Bob Watson 86, Cesar Cedeno 82) and four of them had more than 20 homers (May 29, Wynn 24, Rader 22, Cedeno 22). Wynn set a team record with 117 runs (five fewer than Morgan scored in leading the majors for the Reds) as the Astros led the N.L. in scoring with 708 runs. Cedeno, 21, batted .320, scored 103 runs and had 55 steals. Larry Dierker (15-8) and Don Wilson (15-10) were the top pitchers while Dave Roberts, obtained from San Diego, went 12-7. Harry Walker was fired as manager on Aug. 25 with Houston (67-54) trailing the Reds by nine games. His successor was Leo Durocher, 67, who had resigned under pressure from the Cubs a month earlier.

JESUS ALOU

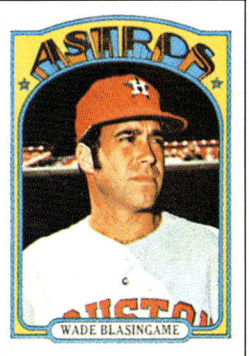
WADE BLASINGAME

CESAR CEDENO

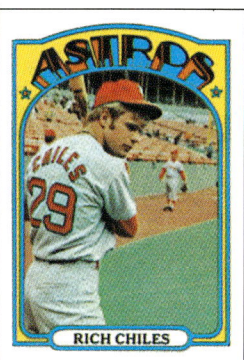
RICH CHILES

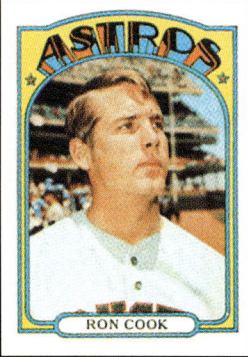
RON COOK

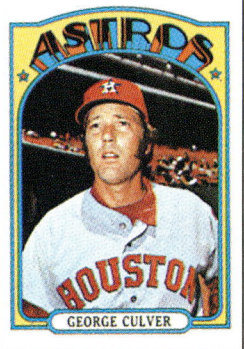
GEORGE CULVER

LARRY DIERKER

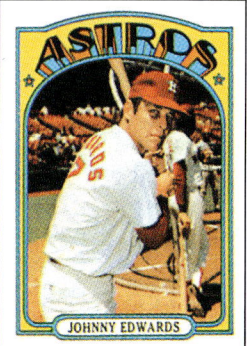
JOHNNY EDWARDS

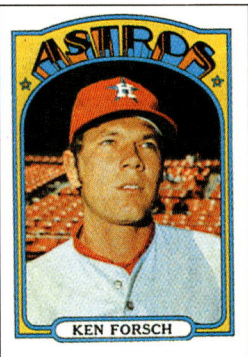

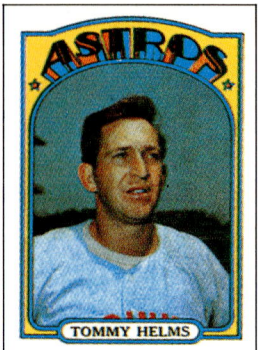
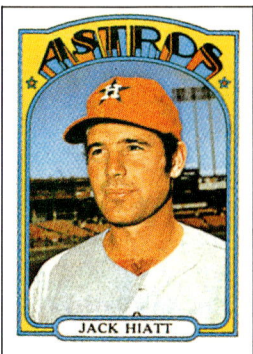

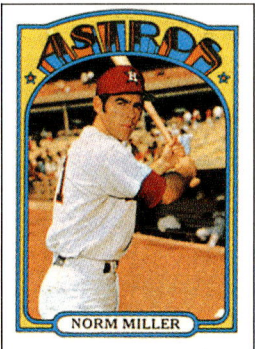

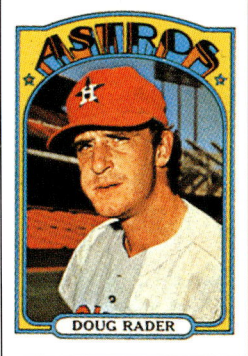
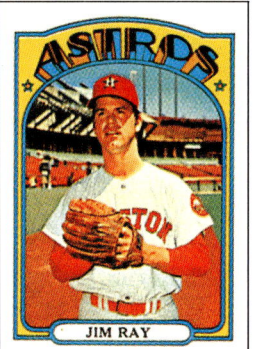
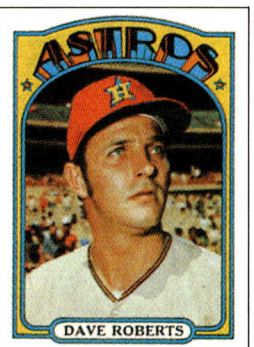

 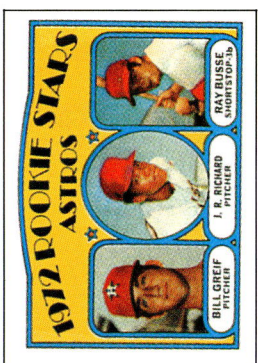  

1973

Cesar Cedeno became the first player in history to steal 50 bases (he had 56 this year) and hit 20 home runs (25) in successive seasons. The fleet centerfielder also was second in the N.L. in batting at .320. Bob Watson, moved to leftfield when Lee May was acquired, was fifth in the league at .312 and scored 97 runs while driving in 94. May was a third big bat (.270, 28 homers, 105 RBIs). He hit three homers in one game and had a 21-game hitting streak. Shortstop Roger Metzger led the majors with 14 triples and won a Gold Glove. But this hitting wasn't enough to make the Astros contenders as they came in fourth at 82-80, 17 games behind the Reds. Larry Dierker made only three starts because of shoulder problems. Dave Roberts (17-11, 2.86 ERA, six shutouts) and Jerry Reuss (16-13, 3.74) were the top pitchers. Reuss was traded on Halloween to Pittsburgh for catcher Milt May. Also playing his final season for Houston was Jimmy Wynn (.220, 20 homers, 55 RBIs), who was traded to the Dodgers for Claude Osteen and a minor leaguer. Wynn left with a club-record 223 homers. It also was the last season for manager Leo Durocher, who resigned.

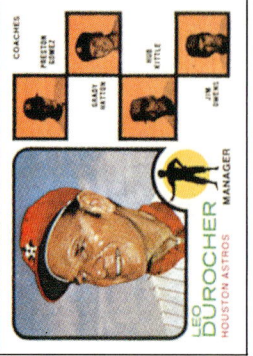

   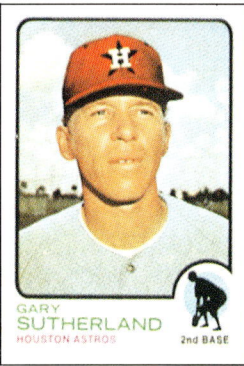

1974

The Astros under new manager Preston Gomez were knocked out of contention early, losing 10 straight in May. They came in fourth with an 81-81 record, 21 games behind the Dodgers. Two rookies who made impressions were rightfielder Greg Gross (.314, third in the N.L.) and catcher-first baseman Cliff Johnson (five pinch-hit home runs). Cesar Cedeno had another productive season (.269, 26 homers, 102 RBIs, 56 steals), as did Lee May (.268, 24 homers, 85 RBIs). Ken Forsch became the ace of the bullpen (8-7, 10 saves, 2.80 ERA) while the three best starters were Tom Griffin (14-10, 3.54), Larry Dierker (11-10, 2.89) and Don Wilson (11-13, 3.07). Wilson had a no-hitter for eight innings against the Reds when he was removed for a pinch-hitter because the Astros trailed 2-1. Reliever Mike Cosgrove allowed a single in the ninth inning to Tony Perez. The Phils' Mike Schmidt became the only player to hit an overhead speaker in fair territory (leftfield) in the Astrodome. He was held to a single.

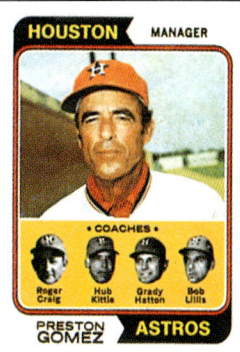

1975

Tragedy struck the Astros before the season when Don Wilson was found dead in his garage, a victim of monoxide poisoning. The Astros had the worst record (64-97) in their history as they finished last, 43½ games behind the Reds. Preston Gomez was fired as manager on Aug. 19 with the team at 47-80. Bill Virdon, who had been fired as Yankees manager 19 days earlier, replaced him. The Astros split 34 games under him. Bob Watson was fifth in the N.L. in batting at .324 and led the Astros with 85 RBIs. Cliff Johnson paced the team with 20 homers—in only 340 at-bats. Cedar Cedeno hit .288 and stole 50 bases. Outfielder Wilbur Howard batted .283 and had 32 steals. Pitching was Houston's problem. No regular starter had an ERA under 4.00 and only two pitchers won more than eight games: Larry Dierker (14-16) and J.R. Richard (12-10), who was pitching regularly for the first time. Tal Smith became GM, replacing Spec Richardson.

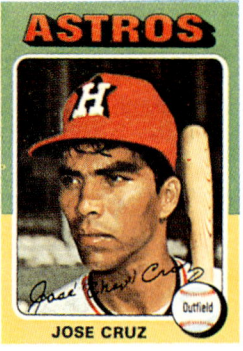

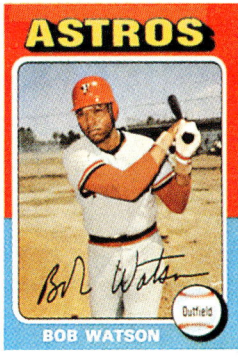

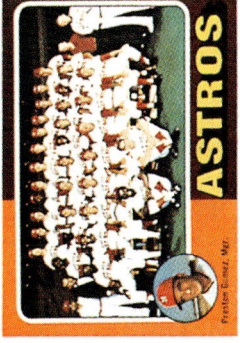

1976

J.R. Richard became the Astros' second 20-game winner as he went 20-15 with a 2.75 ERA in 291 innings. Larry Dierker, the first 20-game winner, was the Astros' only other double-figure winner, going 13-14 with a 3.69 ERA. Dierker, who had an eight-inning perfect game against the Mets in 1966 and lost 1-0 in the ninth, no-hit Montreal on July 9. Dierker, a 13-year veteran with Houston, was traded to the Cards in November. Ken Forsch had 19 saves (tied for second in the N.L.) and a 2.15 ERA. The key everyday players were Bob Watson (.313, 16 homers, 102 RBIs), Cesar Cedeno (.297, 18 homers, 83 RBIs, 58 steals, the last of five straight Gold Gloves) and outfielder Jose Cruz (.303, 28 steals). In Bill Virdon's first full season as manager, the Astros improved to 80-82 as they finished third, 22 games behind the Reds. The team was purchased by General Electric Credit Corp. and Ford Motor Credit Co. from Judge Roy Hofheinz.

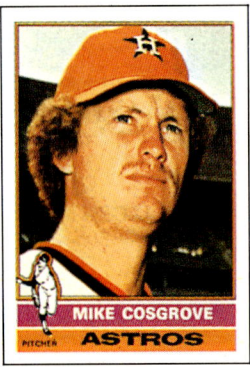

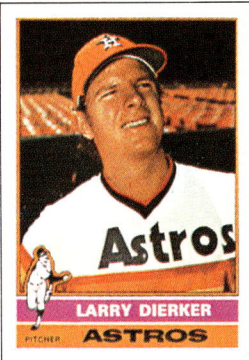

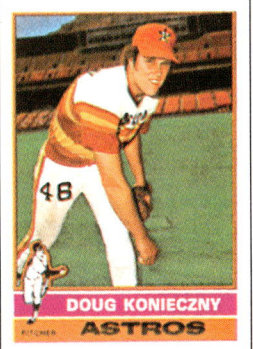

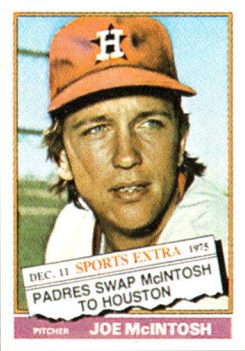

1977

C the Astros run. Three players whose last name began with C stole more than 40 bases as Cesar Cedeno had a club-record 61, Jose Cruz 44 and third baseman Enos Cabell 42. The three C's also got A's in other offensive departments. Cedeno batted .279 and scored 92 runs, Cruz hit .299 with 87 runs and 87 RBIs, and Cabell batted .282 and scored a team-leading 101 runs. Bob Watson set a team-record with 110 RBIs and led the team with 22 homers. Rookie leftfielder Terry Puhl's .301 average was the highest on the team. J.R. Richard was the Astros' big pitcher with his 18-12 record and 2.97 ERA. Joe Niekro went 13-8 and Joaquin Andujar, in his second season, had an 11-8 record despite missing almost two months because of a hamstring injury. The Astros finished third at 81-81, 17 games behind the Dodgers.

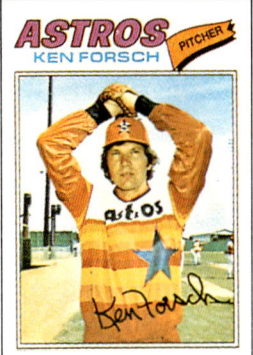

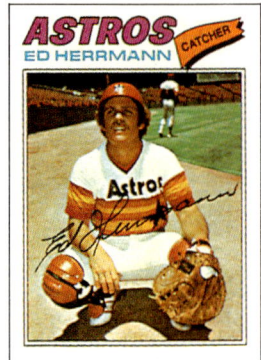

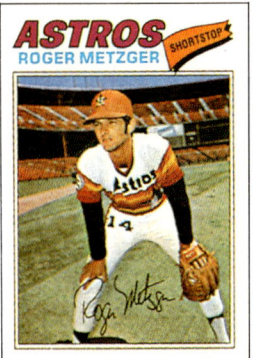
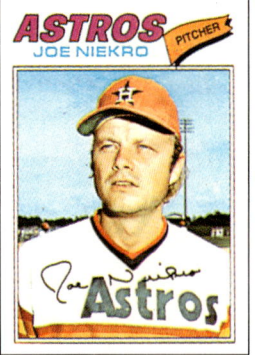

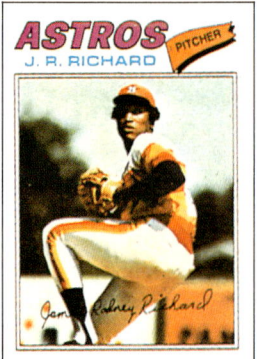
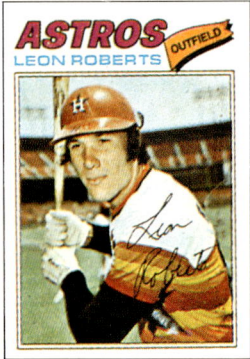

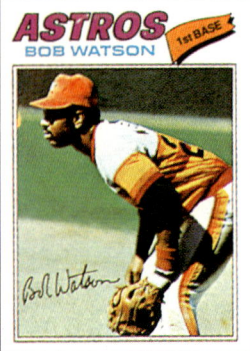

1978

J.R. Richard became the first righthander in the N.L. history to strike out 300 batters (he whiffed 303). He went 18-11 with a 3.11 ERA in 275 innings. But the Astros only had one other pitcher with a winning record (Ken Forsch at 10-6) as they dropped back to fifth place at 74-88, 21 games behind the Dodgers. One problem was that they didn't have a catcher. Another was that they didn't have a shortstop after sending Roger Metzger to the Giants on June 15. Another was that the next day Cesar Cedeno suffered knee ligament damage and was operated on the following day. He didn't play again until the final weekend. There were a few bright spots. Enos Cabell set a team record with 195 hits in batting .295. Jose Cruz was third in the league in batting at .315 and drove in a team-high 83 runs. Terry Puhl and Bob Watson both hit .289, and Watson led the team with 14 homers.

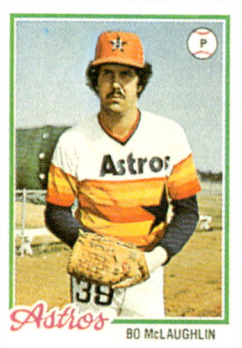

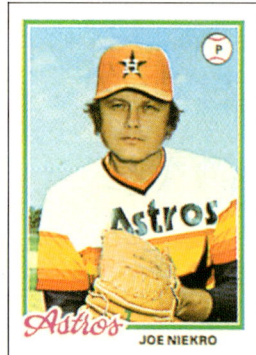

1979

On July 4 the Astros were 52-31 and 10 ½ games ahead of the Reds (41-41). But the Astros went 37-42 the rest of the way to finish 89-73, in second place, 1 ½ games behind Cincinnati. J.R. Richard led the majors in strikeouts when he fanned a club-record 313. He also led the N.L. in ERA at 2.71 in his 18-13 season. Joe Niekro set a club record for victories in going 21-11. Ken Forsch went 11-6 with his first victory being a no-hitter of the Braves in the second game of the season. His brother Bob had pitched a no-hitter for St. Louis in 1978 and they are the only brother combination to pitch no-hitters. Joaquin Andujar went 12-12. The Astros became the first team to have four different N.L. pitchers of the month. However, the Astros didn't have much power as their 49 homers were one more than major league home-run leader Dave Kingman of the Cubs hit. The Astros relied on speed, leading the N.L. in steals with 190 as Enos Cabell had 37, Jose Cruz 36, and Terry Puhl and Cesar Cedeno 30 each. John McMullen became the principal owner, buying the team from the Ford Motor Credit Co., which had bought out the General Electric Credit Corp. in 1978.

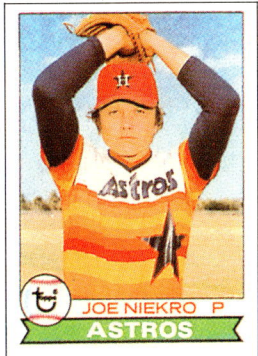

 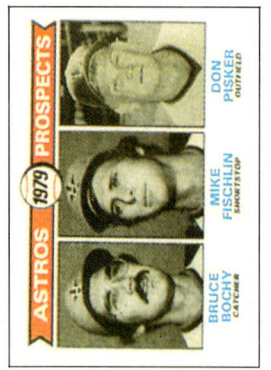 

1980

The Astros went into the final three games in L.A. with a three-game lead over the Dodgers. They lost all three. But the next day, Joe Niekro's pitching and Art Howe's four RBIs led Houston to a 7-1 victory in the playoff game. In finishing 93-70, the Astros attracted a team-record 2,278,217 fans. The playoff series between the Astros and Phils was perhaps the most exciting in history. The Astros led two games to one before the Phils came back to win games four and five, both in 10 innings. The Astros led the majors with a 3.10 ERA. The staff had been strengthened in the offseason with the signing of free-agent Nolan Ryan to a four-year contract worth $4.5 million. The fireballing righthander went 11-10 with a 3.35 ERA. Niekro led the staff with a 20-12 record while Vern Ruhle went 12-4 with a 2.38 ERA. But the staff was struck by tragedy on July 30. J.R. Richard, who was 10-4 with a 1.89 ERA, collapsed after a workout. He had suffered a stroke and had emergency surgery to remove a blood clot behind the right collarbone which threatened his life. He never pitched again in the majors. President and GM Tal Smith, who was named Executive of the Year, was fired by owner John McMullen after the season for "philosophical differences." Al Rosen replaced Smith.

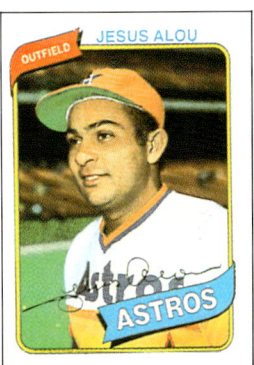

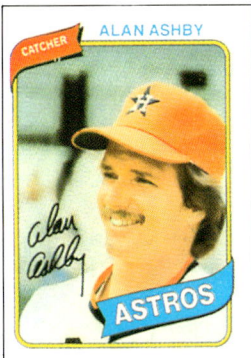
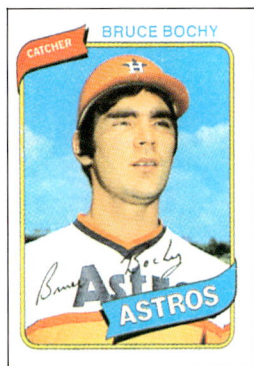

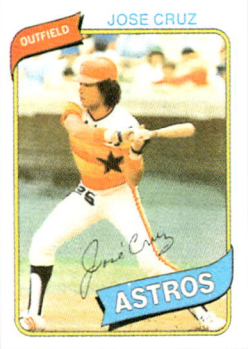
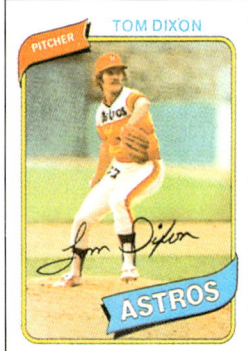

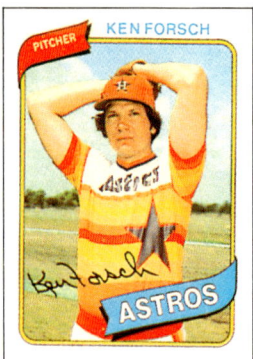
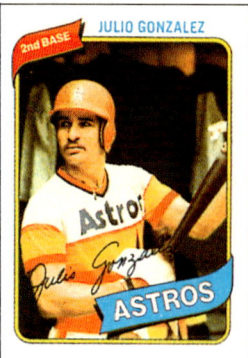
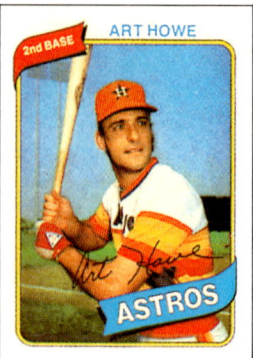
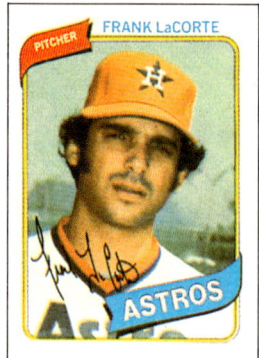
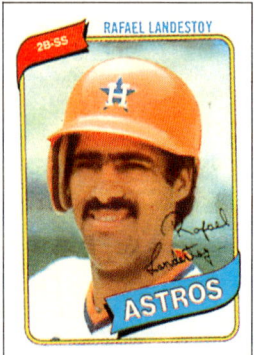

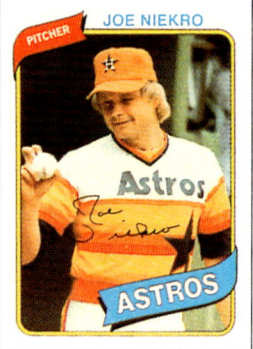

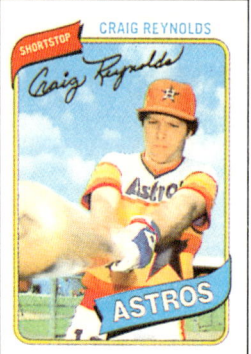

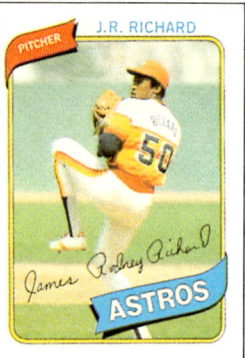

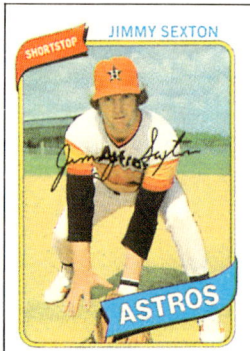

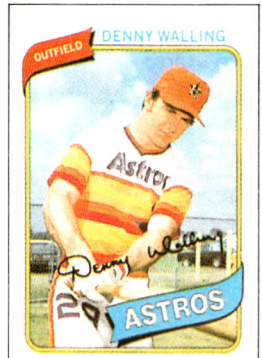

1981

A 50-day players' strike caused the season to be split into two sessions. The Astros finished third in the first half at 28-29, eight games behind the Dodgers. But they won the second half at 33-20, finishing 1½ games ahead of the Reds. They won the first two games of the divisional playoff series with the Dodgers at home but then lost the final three in L.A. Nolan Ryan (11-5) became the first player ever to pitch five no-hitters when he no-hit the Dodgers on Sept. 26. (His first four were with the Angels.) He also won his first ERA title (1.69). Bob Knepper, obtained from the Giants the previous December in a trade for Enos Cabell, was outstanding (9-5, 2.18 ERA). Don Sutton, signed as a free agent (four years, $3.5 million), went 11-9 with a 2.60 ERA and Joe Niekro was 9-9 with a 2.82 ERA. Jose Cruz was the only Astro to hit more than five homers (he had 13). Despite a second-half slump, Art Howe led the team with a .296 average and set a team record with his 23-game batting streak. Cesar Cedeno was fined $5,000 by the N.L. for going into the stands in Atlanta and fighting with a fan. He was traded to the Reds for Ray Knight in December.

  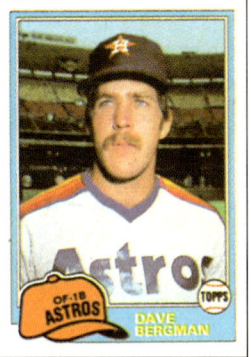 

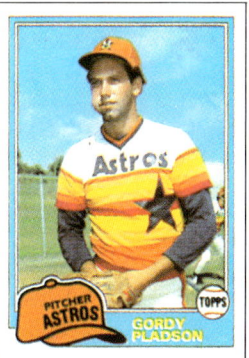
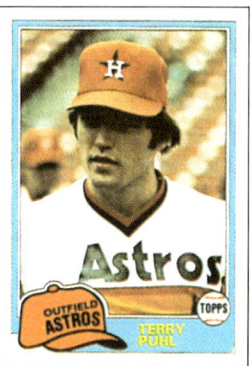

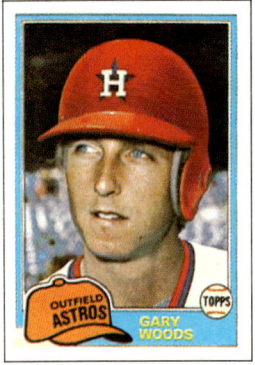

1982

With little hitting—the Astros were last in the N.L. in batting at .247—the Astros fell from being contenders. On Aug. 10, with the Astros 49-62, Bill Virdon was fired as manager. He was replaced by Bob Lillis, a coach with the Astros since 1973 and the first Houston team MVP in 1962. Under him the Astros went 28-23 to finish 77-85, in fifth place, 12 games behind the Braves. On Aug. 30 they traded veteran Don Sutton (13-8, 3.00 ERA) to the Brewers for three minor leaguers, including two (outfielder Kevin Bass and pitcher Frank DiPino) who would be considerable assets in the future. While Joe Niekro (17-12, 2.47 ERA was second in the N.L.) and Nolan Ryan (16-12, 3.16) again had good seasons, Bob Knepper faltered (5-15). Second baseman Phil Garner, obtained from Pittsburgh during the previous August for three minor leaguers (one was Johnny Ray), led the Astros with 13 homers and 83 RBIs. Shortstop Dickie Thon, acquired from the Angels for Ken Forsch in April 1981, showed his potential by hitting .276 (second on the team to Ray Knight's .294) and stealing a team-leading 37 bases.

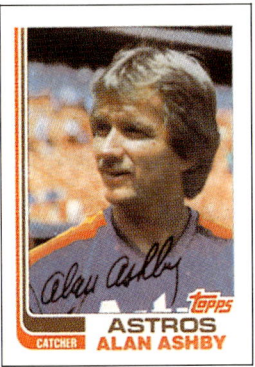 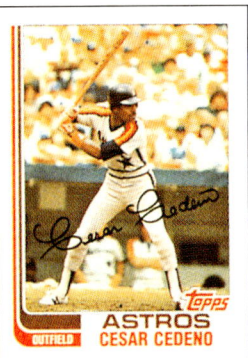 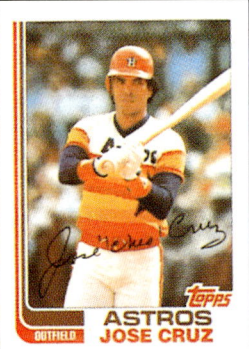 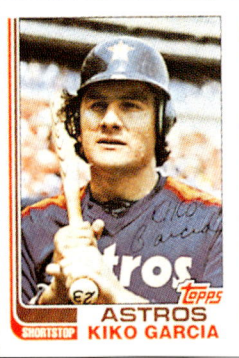

 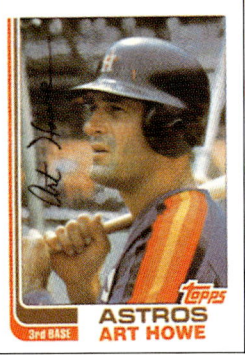  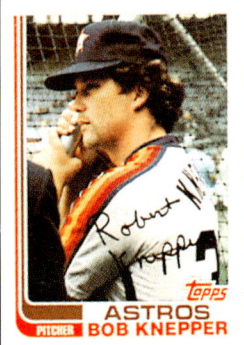

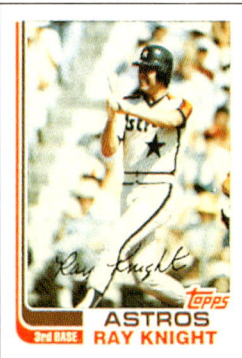
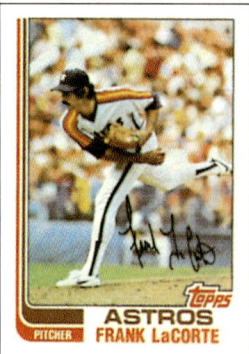

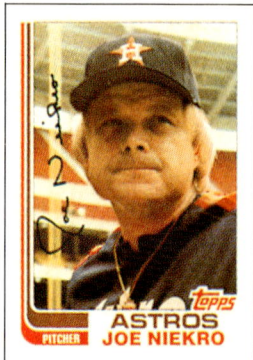

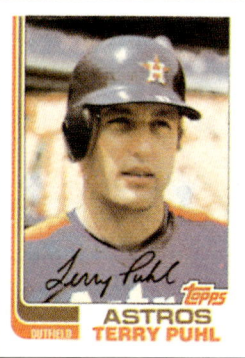

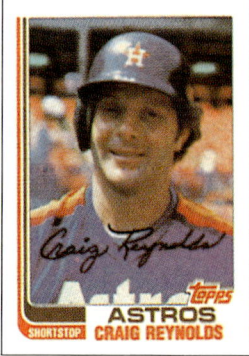

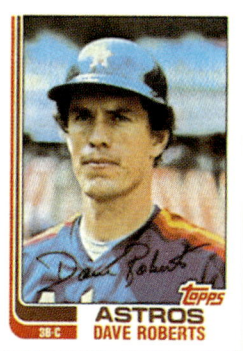

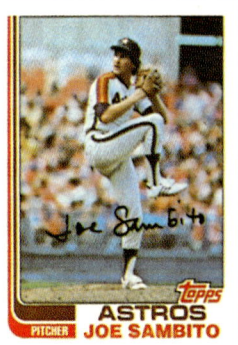

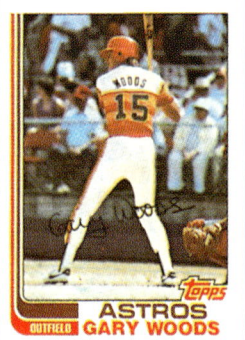
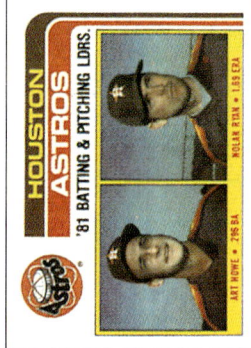
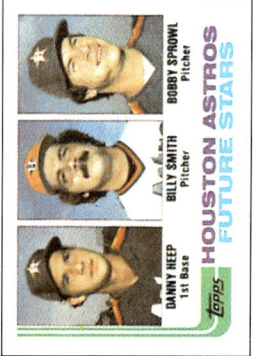

1983

The Astros tied the N.L. record by losing their first nine games. However, from then on, they played 17 games over .500 to finish third at 85-77, six games behind the Dodgers. On June 3 they were 13½ games out. Nolan Ryan broke Walter Johnson's 56-year-old strikeout record when he fanned the 3,509th batter of his career. Ryan (14-9, 2.98 ERA) and Joe Niekro (15-14, 3.48) were joined in the starting rotation by Mike Scott (10-6, 3.72), acquired in the offseason from the Mets for sub outfielder Danny Heep. The bullpen was headed by two talented rookies—Frank DiPino (20 saves, 2.65 ERA) and Bill Dawley (14 saves, 2.82). Dickie Thon became a full-fledged star (.286, 20 homers, 79 RBIs, 81 runs, 34 steals, 18 game-winning hits to lead the N.L.). Jose Cruz was in the batting race until the end (.318 finished third, five points behind winner Bill Madlock) and knocked in 92 runs and stole 30 bases. Ray Knight's .304 average was fifth in the N.L.

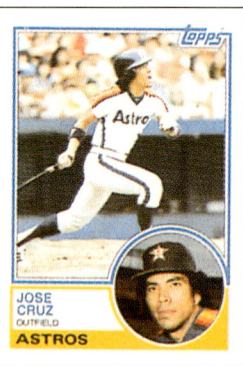

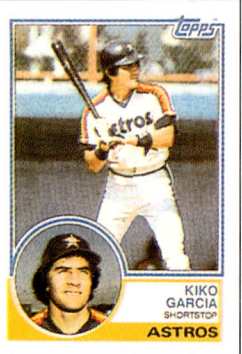

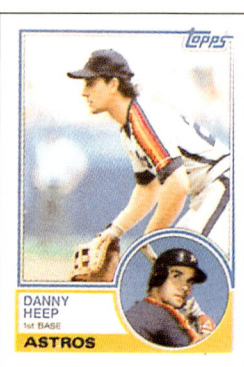

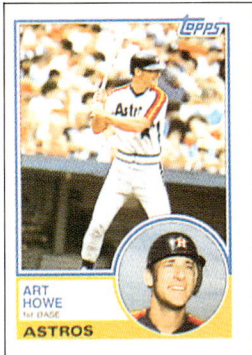

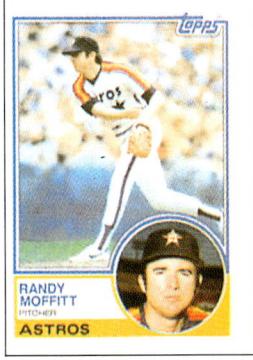

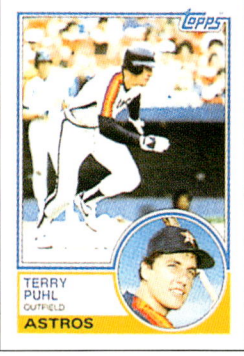

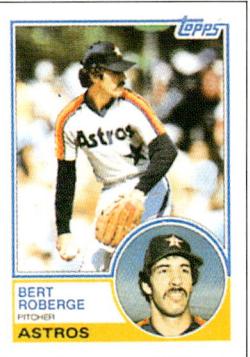

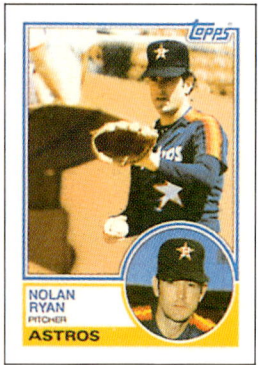

1984

Another tragic blow was suffered by the Astros when Dickie Thon was beaned by the Mets' Mike Torrez in the fifth game of the season, suffering severe damage near the left eye. Blurred vision sidelined him the rest of the year. The Astros started poorly again—this time 1-6—but this season they never recovered. They finished 80-82, tied for second with the Braves, 12 games behind the Padres. Joe Niekro made the most starts in the N.L. (38), compiling a record with a 3.04 ERA. Bob Knepper bounced back from 5-15 and 6-13 seasons to go 15-10 with a 3.20 ERA. Nolan Ryan, though injured three times, went 12-11 with a 3.04 ERA. In the bullpen Frank DiPino had 14 saves while Bill Dawley went 11-4 with a 1.93 ERA. Jose Cruz led the Astros in batting (.312, sixth in the N.L.), runs (96), homers (13), RBIs (95) and steals (22). Terry Puhl hit .301 while centerfielder Jerry Mumphrey batted .290 with 83 RBIs.

 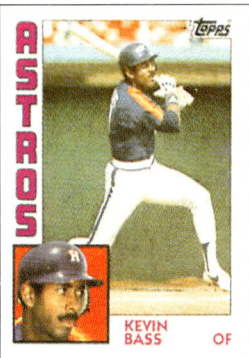  

 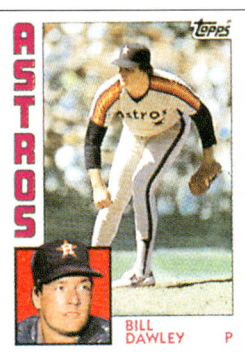 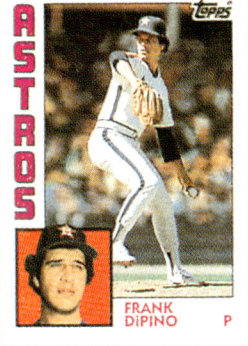 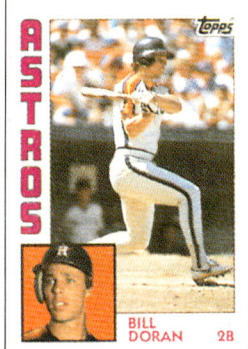

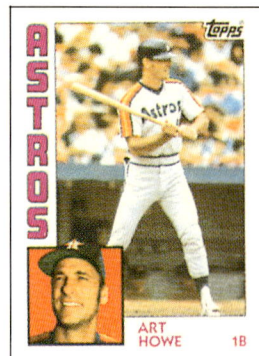
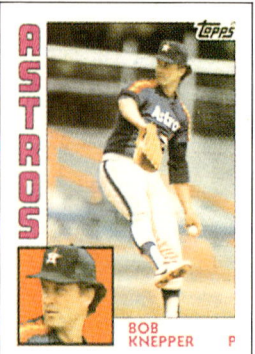
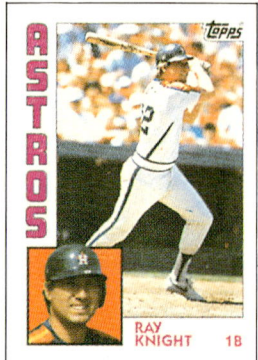
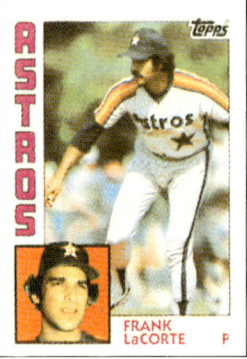
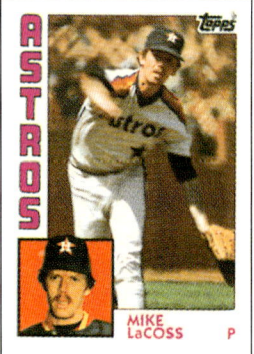

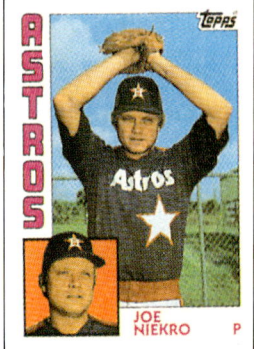
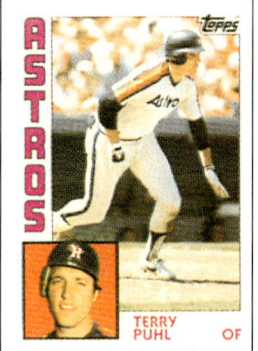
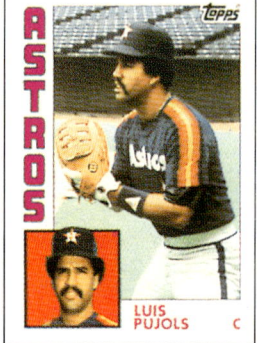
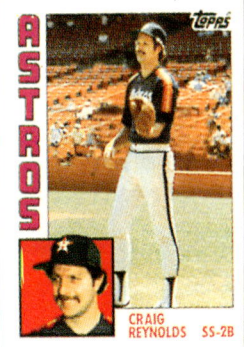

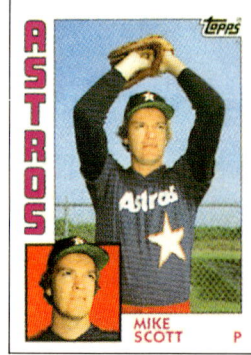

 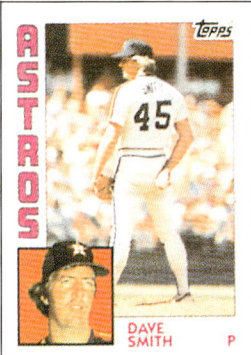 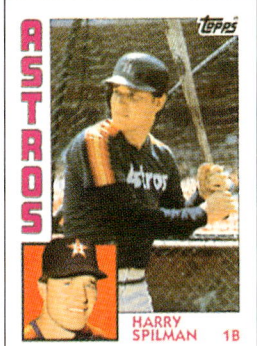 

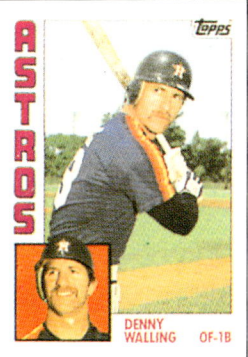 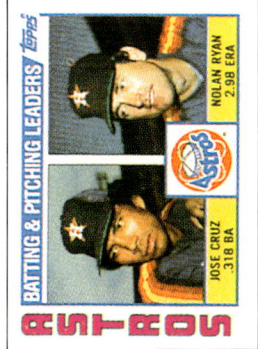

1985

On June 12 the Astros were in the pennant race, 2½ games behind the Dodgers. On June 23, they were out of it, having lost six straight to the Dodgers in a 10-game stretch. They finished tied for third with the Padres at 83-79, 12 games behind the Dodgers. Team president and GM Al Rosen quit in September—becoming GM of the Giants—before he was fired by John McMullen. He was replaced by Dick Wagner, whose first move was to trade 40-year-old Joe Niekro (9-12, 3.72 ERA) to the Yankees for three minor leaguers. Niekro left with a club record 144 victories. After the season, McMullen and Wagner fired Bob Lillis as manager. Dickie Thon, still having vision problems, played only 84 games, hitting .251. Nolan Ryan (10-12) became the first pitcher to strike out 4,000 batters when he fanned Danny Heep. He also tied Tom Seaver's record of 10 seasons with at least 200 strikeouts. Mike Scott mastered the split-finger fastball and went 18-8 with a 3.29 ERA. Dave Smith was the star of the bullpen (9-5, 27 saves, 2.27 ERA). Jose Cruz (.300) stroked his 2,000th hit during his third straight .300 season. First baseman Glenn Davis, called up from the minors in mid-June, set a Houston rookie record with 20 homers—in only 100 games.

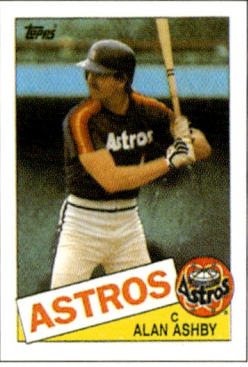

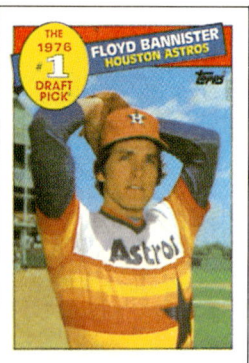

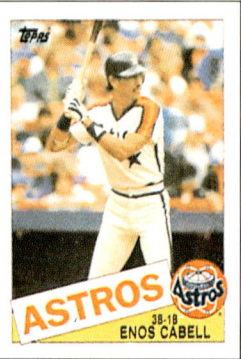

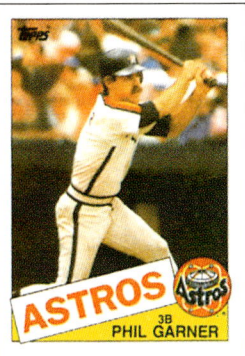
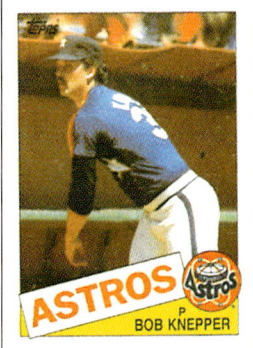

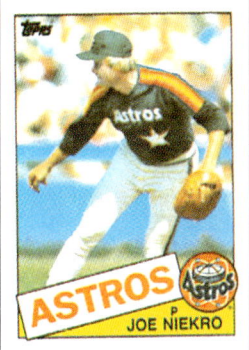

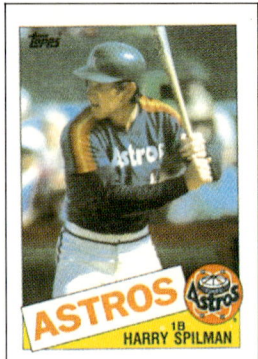

1986

Under Hal Lanier, in his first major league managing job, the Astros went into orbit, winning the N.L. West by 10 games over Cincinnati as they went a club-record 96-66. Mike Scott came into his own, leading the majors in strikeouts (306), ERA (2.22) and innings (275⅓). He had an 18-10 record, including a no-hitter of the Giants in the Astros' division clincher. He added two more victories in the playoffs against the Mets (allowing one run in 18 innings), but the Astros lost the other four games in a breathtaking series that included a 12-inning Game 5 and 16-inning finale. Bob Knepper was second on the team in wins (17-12, 3.14 ERA) and tied with Scott for most shutouts in the league (five). Nolan Ryan went 12-8 and rookie lefthander Jim Deshaies 12-5. Deshaies, obtained in the Joe Niekro deal the previous September, set a 20th-century record by striking out the first eight batters in a game (against the Dodgers). Dave Smith set a team record with 33 saves, third in the N.L. Glenn Davis supplied the power with 31 homers (tied for second in the N.L.) and 101 RBIs (fourth). Rightfielder Kevin Bass batted .311 with 20 homers, 79 RBIs and 22 steals. Second baseman Bill Doran led the club in runs (92) and steals (42).

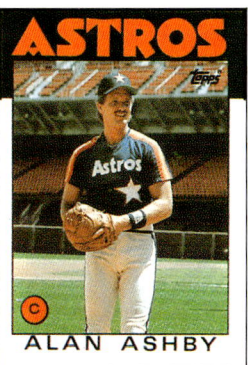
ALAN ASHBY

MARK BAILEY

KEVIN BASS

JEFF CALHOUN

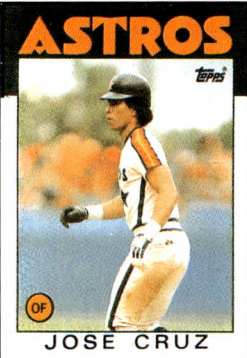
JOSE CRUZ

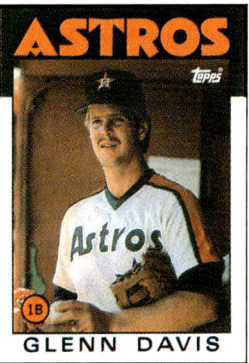
GLENN DAVIS

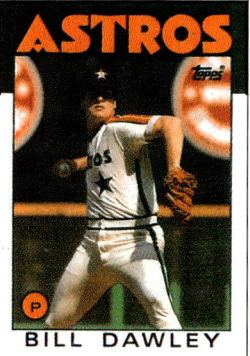
BILL DAWLEY

FRANK DiPINO

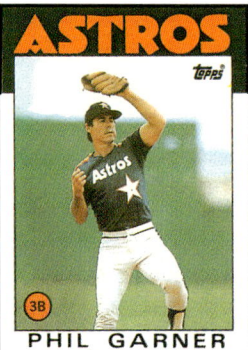
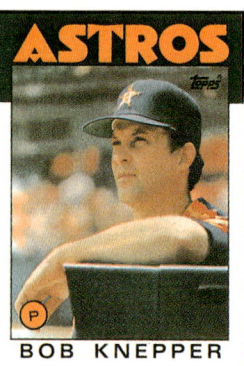
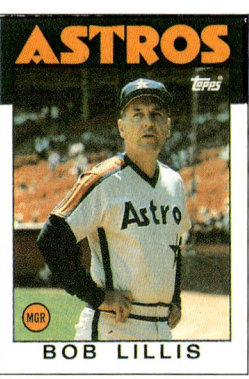

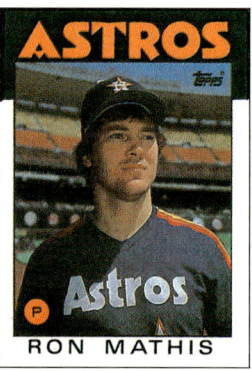
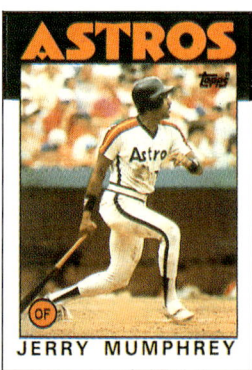

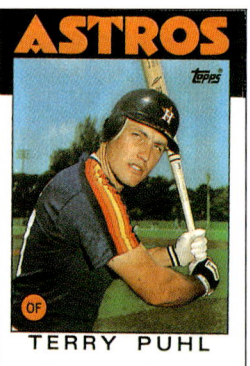

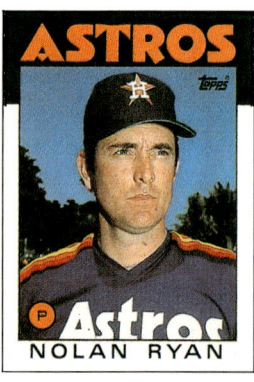

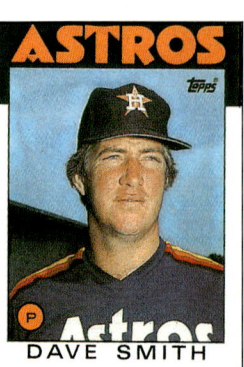
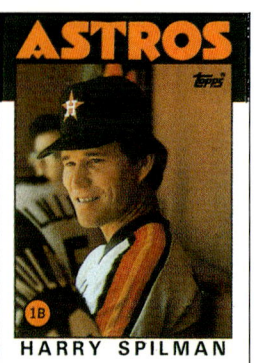

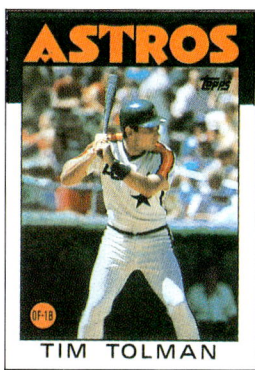 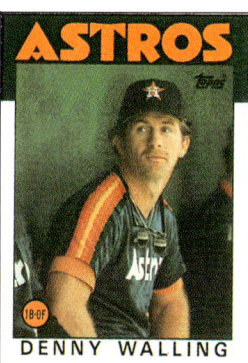 

1987

Nolan Ryan can tell you what kind of a year it was for the Houston Astros — strange.

Ryan led the National League in strikeouts with 270 in slightly less than 212 innings and also had the league's best ERA (2.76) but still finished with an 8-16 record.

When that kind of performance produces that sort of results, it's clear to see why the Astros were unable to defend their West division title.

Mike Scott finished second to Ryan among the N.L. pitchers in strikeouts with 233 but had what was considered an "off" year for him: a 16-13 record with a 3.23 ERA.

Lefthander Jim Deshaies was 11-6, but was limited to 26 appearances by injury.

While not grabbing headlines like some of his bullpen compatriots on other teams, Dave Smith was just short of spectacular again with 24 saves, 73 strikeouts in 60 innings, only 39 hits allowed and no home runs against for the season.

Gerald Young began the season in the minors but was the regular center fielder by season's end and finished with a .321 average.

Billy Hatcher moved to left but continued his heavy production with a .296 average, 11 homers, 63 RBI and 53 stolen bases (third highest total in the league).

Another rookie, Ken Caminiti, provided some of the best defensive play at third base seen by Astros fans in many years and was selected as the league's Player of the Week in his first week in the lineup.

Slugging first baseman Glen Davis again led the Astros in home runs with 27 and runs batted in with 93 while hitting .251. Kevin Bass had 19 homers and 85 RBI to go with his .284 average.

Catcher Alan Ashby turned in another fine season with a .288 average, 14 homers and 63 RBI.

Second baseman Bill Doran remained among the league's premiere players at his position with a .283 average, 16 homers and 79 RBI (third best on the club) while Denny Walling also hit .283.

Characteristic of the way the season went for Houston was the fact that the Astros played 54 one-run games, more than any other team in the division. Unfortunately, the Astros won 25 of them and lost 29.

Those 29 one-run losses made the difference in the 1987 season as the Astros finished third, 14 games behind the division-leading San Francisco Giants.

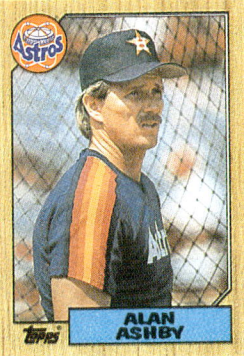

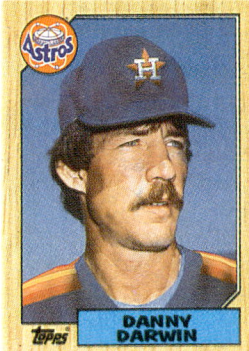

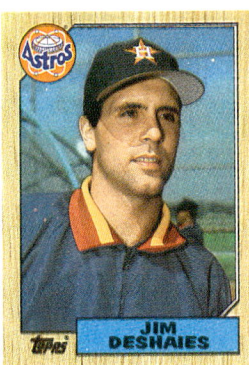
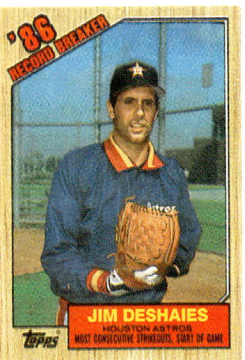

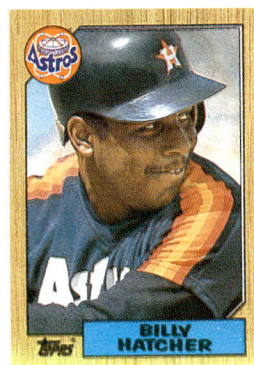

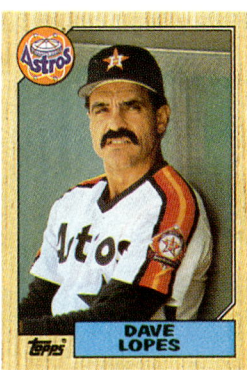
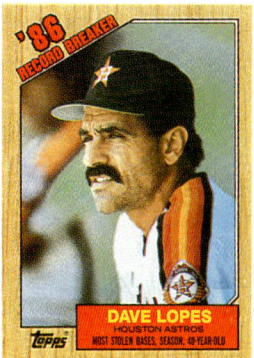
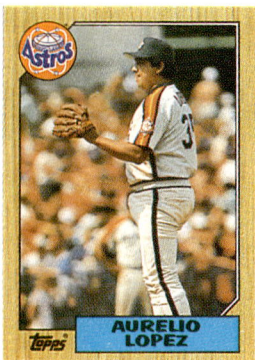
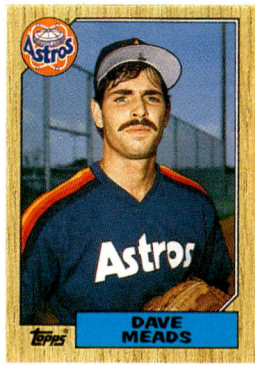
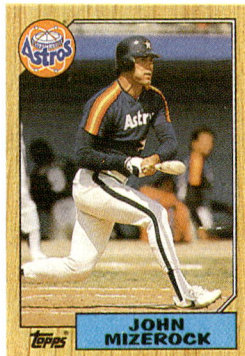
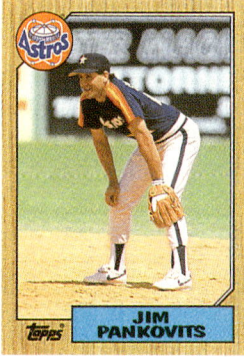

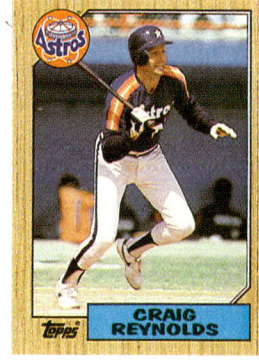

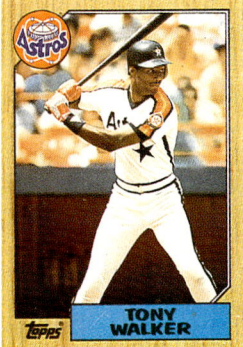

1988

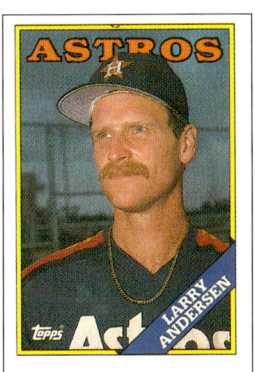 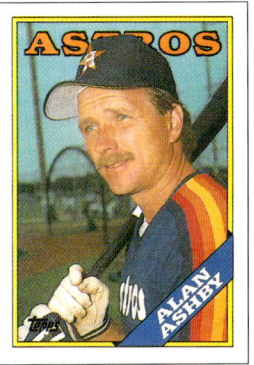 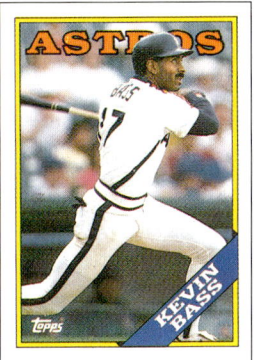 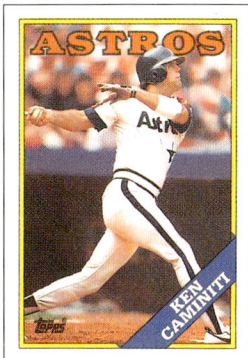
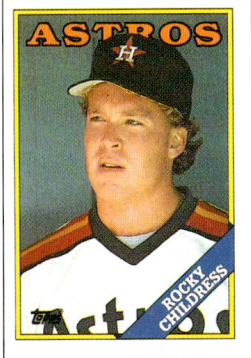  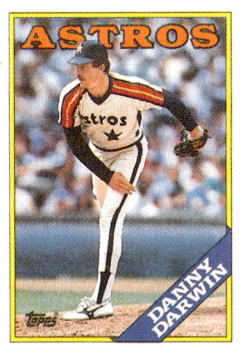 
  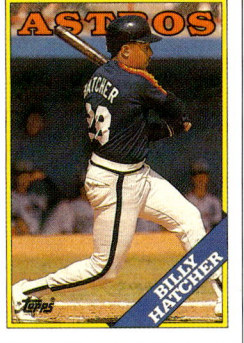 

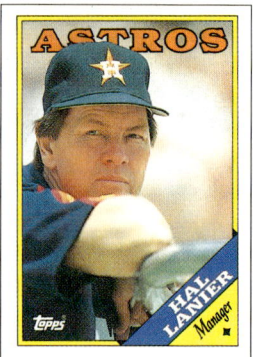
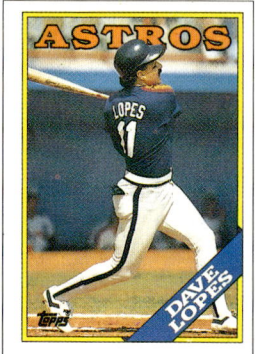
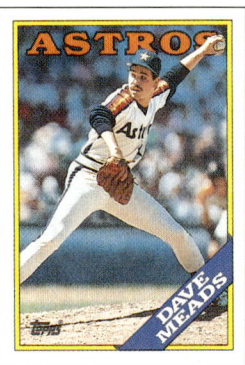
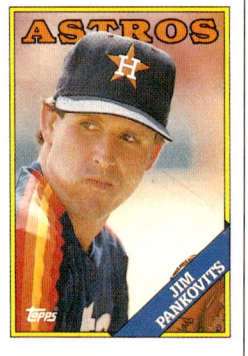

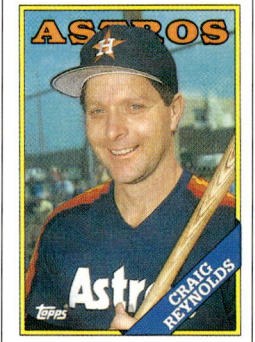

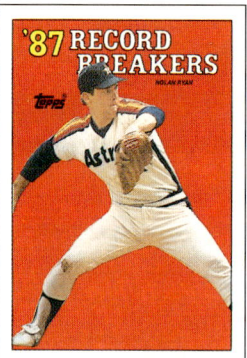

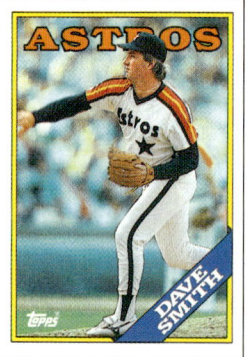

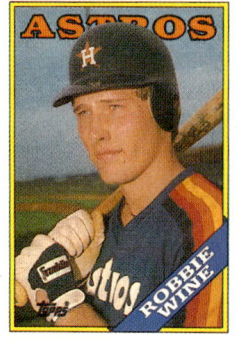
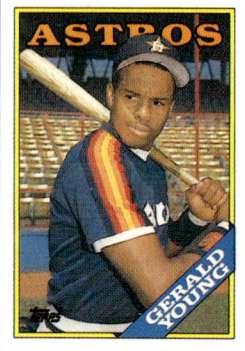

Salute to NOLAN RYAN

As a power pitcher, Nolan Ryan has no peer. Major league baseball's all-time strikeout king, Ryan continues to blow fastballs past opposing hitters at an age when most of his hard-throwing contemporaries have either abandoned their fastballs for less demanding varieties of pitches or have retired from the game all together.

Ryan's five no-hitters and over 4,500 career strikeouts alone are impressive enough records. Both rank in a class with such legendary marks as Joe DiMaggio's 56-game hitting streak or Roger Maris' 61 homers. But it is his longevity, an uncommon trait among the fraternity of flamethrowers, that makes him much more special.

In his remarkable career, Ryan has averaged better than one strikeout per inning pitched (9.46 per 9 innings). Sandy Koufax is the only other pitcher in history to average better than one whiff per nine innings pitched, but Koufax' career ended after only 2,325 innings while Ryan's has lasted more than 2,000 innings longer. In 1987, at age 40, he averaged an incredible 11.48, the highest of his career.

Ryan began his major league career in 1966 as a reliever with the New York Mets. Blessed with a blazing fastball, Ryan was an overlooked commodity on a staff that also featured Tom Seaver and Jerry Koosman. It wasn't until he was dealt to the California Angels in late 1971 that Ryan found his niche.

The "Alvin Express," as he came to be known, stormed through the American League, fanning 329 in his first season and in 1973 broke Koufax' major league record with an incredible 383. Before he was through, Ryan had fanned more than 300 five times in eight seasons with the Angels and had thrown four no-hitters before choosing to return home to Texas and the Astros as a free agent after the 1979 season.

With Houston, Ryan treated the fans to a record-setting fifth no-hitter (again eclipsing Koufax) and to his pursuit of Walter Johnson's all-time strikeout record. That mark fell in 1983 and in 1985 he pushed past the 4,000 strikeout barrier. Then in 1987 on a night that saw him fan a major league season-high 16 San Francisco Giants, Ryan reached 4,500.

After battling a sore elbow in 1986, Ryan decided against major surgery and rested the ailing joint. He then proceeded to prove the wisdom of his choice by putting together a remarkable set of numbers in 1987, proving once and for all that he is the greatest power pitcher in baseball history.

He led the majors in strikeouts for the sixth time in his career and the first time in the National League. His 270 whiffs were his highest total in 10 seasons and set a record for pitchers 40 years or older. With his league-topping total, he joined Rube Waddell and Jim Bunning as the only pitchers ever to lead both leagues in K's. He also tied for the major league lead with a 2.76 ERA. He fanned 10 or more in 12 of his 34 starts, raising his career total to 174 — yet another major league record.

COLLECTORS' CORNER

1951: Blue Back of Johnny Mize (50) lists for $25 . . . Red Back of Duke Snider (38) lists for $18 . . . Complete set of 9 Team Cards lists for $900 . . . Complete set of 11 Connie Mack All-Stars lists for $2750 with Babe Ruth and Lou Gehrig listing for $700 each . . . Current All-Stars of Jim Konstanty, Robin Roberts and Eddie Stanky list for $4000 each . . . Complete set lists for $14,250.

1952: Mickey Mantle (311) is unquestionably the most sought-after post-war gum card, reportedly valued at $6,500-plus . . . Ben Chapman (391) is photo of Sam Chapman . . . Complete set lists in excess of $36,000.

1953: Mickey Mantle (82) and Willie Mays (244) list for $1,500 each . . . Set features first TOPPS card of Hall-of-Famer Whitey Ford (207) and only TOPPS card of Hall-of-Famer Satchel Paige (220). Pete Runnels (219) is photo of Don Johnson . . . Complete set lists for $9,500.

1954: Ted Williams is depicted on two cards (1 and 250) . . . Set features rookie cards of Hank Aaron (128), Ernie Banks (94) and Al Kaline (201) . . . Card of Aaron lists for $650 . . . Card of Willie Mays (90) lists for $200 . . . Complete set lists for $5,500.

1955: Set features rookie cards of Sandy Koufax (123), Harmon Killebrew (124) and Roberto Clemente (164) . . . The Clemente and Willie Mays (194) cards list for $425 each . . . Complete set lists for $3,900.

1956: Set features rookie cards of Hall-of-Famers Will Harridge (1), Warren Giles (2), Walter Alston (8) and Luis Aparicio (292) . . . Card of Mickey Mantle (135) lists for $650 . . . Card of Willie Mays (130) lists for $125 . . . Complete set lists for $4,000 . . . The Team Cards are found both dated (1955) and undated and are valued at $15 (dated) and more . . . There are two unnumbered Checklist Cards valued high.

1957: Set features rookie cards of Don Drysdale (18), Frank Robinson (35) and Brooks Robinson (328) . . . A reversal of photo negative made Hank Aaron (20) appear as a left-handed batter . . . Card of Mickey Mantle (95) lists for $600 . . . Cards of Brooks Robinson and Sandy Koufax (302) list for $275 each . . . Complete set lists for $4,800.

1958: Set features first TOPPS cards of Casey Stengel (475) and Stan Musial (476) . . . Mike McCormick (37) is photo of Ray Monzant . . . Milt Bolling (188) is photo of Lou Berberet . . . Bob Smith (226) is photo of Bobby Gene Smith . . . Card of Mickey Mantle (150) lists for $400 . . . Card of Ted Williams (1) lists for $325 . . . Complete set lists for $4,800.

1959: In a notable error, Lou Burdette (440) is shown posing as a left-handed pitcher . . . Set features rookie card of Bob Gibson (514) . . . Ralph Lumenti (316) is photo of Camilo Pascual . . . Card of Gibson lists for $200 . . . Card of Mickey Mantle (10) lists for $300 . . . Complete set lists for $3,000.

1960: A run of 32 consecutively numbered rookie cards (117-148) includes the first card of Carl Yastrzemski (148) . . . J.C. Martin (346) is photo of Gary Peters . . . Gary Peters (407) is photo of J.C. Martin . . . Card of Yastrzemski lists for $150 . . . Card of Mickey Mantle (350) lists for $300 . . . Complete set lists for $2,600.

1961: The Warren Spahn All-Star (589) should have been numbered 587 . . . Set features rookie cards of Billy Williams (141) and Juan Marichal (417) . . . Dutch Dotterer (332) is photo of his brother, Tommy . . . Card of Mickey Mantle (300) lists for $200 . . . Card of Carl Yastrzemski (287) lists for $90 . . . Complete set lists for $3,600.

1962: Set includes special Babe Ruth feature (135-144) . . . some Hal Reniff cards numbered 139 should be 159 . . . Set features rookie card of Lou Brock (387) . . . Gene Freese (205) is shown posing as a left-handed batter . . . Card of Mickey Mantle (200) lists for $325 . . . Card of Carl Yastrzemski (425) lists for $125 . . . Complete set lists for $3,300.

1963: Set features rookie card of Pete Rose (537), which lists for $500-plus . . . Bob Uecker (126) is shown posing as a left-handed batter . . . Don Landrum (113) is photo of Ron Santo . . . Eli Grba (231) is photo of Ryne Duren . . . Card of Mickey Mantle (200) lists for $200 . . . Card of Lou Brock (472) lists for $75 . . . Complete set lists for $2,900.

1964: Set features rookie cards of Richie Allen (243), Tony Conigliaro (287) and Phil Niekro (541) . . . Lou Burdette is again shown posing as a left-handed pitcher . . . Bud Bloomfield (532) is photo of Jay Ward . . . Card of Pete Rose (125) lists for $150 . . . Card of Mickey Mantle (50) lists for $175 . . . Complete set lists for $1,600.

1965: Set features rookie cards of Dave Johnson (473), Steve Carlton (477) and Jim Hunter (526) . . . Lew Krausse (462) is photo of Pete Lovrich . . . Gene Freese (492) is again shown posing as a left-handed batter . . . Cards of Carlton and Pete Rose (207) list for $135 . . . Card of Mickey Mantle (350) lists for $300 . . . Complete set lists for $800.

1966: Set features rookie card of Jim Palmer (126) . . . For the third time (see 1962 and 1965) Gene Freese (319) is shown posing as a left-handed batter . . . Dick Ellsworth (447) is photo of Ken Hubbs (died February 13, 1964) . . . Card of Gaylord Perry (598) lists for $175 . . . Card of Willie McCovey (550) lists for $80 . . . Complete set lists for $2,500.

1967: Set features rookie cards of Rod Carew (569) and Tom Seaver (581) . . . Jim Fregosi (385) is shown posing as a left-handed batter . . . George Korince (72) is photo of James Brown but was later corrected on a second Korince card (526) . . . Card of Carew lists for $150 . . . Card of Maury Wills (570) lists for $65 . . . Complete set lists for $2,500.

1968: Set features rookie cards of Nolan Ryan (177) and Johnny Bench (247) . . . The special feature of The Sporting News All-Stars (361-380) includes eight players in the Hall of Fame . . . Card of Ryan lists for $135 . . . Card of Bench lists for $125 . . . Complete set lists for $1,200.

1969: Set features rookie card of Reggie Jackson (260) . . . There are two poses each for Clay Dalrymple (151) and Donn Clendenon (208) . . . Aurelio Rodriguez (653) is photo of Lenny Garcia (Angels' bat boy) . . . Card of Mickey Mantle (500) lists for $150 . . . Card of Jackson lists for $175 . . . Complete set lists for $1,200.

1970: Set features rookie cards of Vida Blue (21), Thurman Munson (189) and Bill Buckner (286) . . . Also included are two deceased players Miguel Fuentes (88) and Paul Edmondson (414) who died after cards went to press . . . Card of Johnny Bench (660) lists for $75 . . . Card of Pete Rose (580) lists for $75 . . . Complete set lists for $1,000.

1971: Set features rookie card of Steve Garvey (341) . . . the final series (644-752) is found in lesser quantity and includes rookie card (664) of three pitchers named Reynolds (Archie, Bob and Ken) . . . Card of Garvey lists for $65 . . . Card of Pete Rose (100) lists for $45 . . . Complete set lists for $1,000.

1972: There were 16 cards featuring photos of players in their boyhood years . . . Dave Roberts (91) is photo of Danny Coombs . . . Brewers Rookie Card (162) includes photos of Darrell Porter and Jerry Bell, which were reversed . . . Cards of Steve Garvey (686) and Rod Carew (695) list for $60 . . . Card of Pete Rose (559) lists for $50 . . . Complete set lists for $1,000.

1973: A special Home Run Card (1) depicted Babe Ruth, Hank Aaron and Willie Mays . . . Set features rookie card of Mike Schmidt (615) listing for $175 . . . Joe Rudi (360) is photo of Gene Tenace . . . Card of Pete Rose (130) lists for $18 . . . Card of Reggie Jackson (255) lists for $12.50 . . . Complete set lists for $600.

1974: Set features 15 San Diego Padres cards printed as "Washington, N.L." due to report of franchise move, later corrected . . . Also included was a 44-card Traded Series which updated team changes . . . Set features rookie card of Dave Winfield (456) . . . Card of Mike Schmidt (283) lists for $35 . . . Card of Winfield lists for $25 . . . Complete set lists for $325.

1975: Herb Washington (407) is the only card ever published with position "designated runner," featuring only base-running statistics . . . Set features rookie cards of Robin Yount (223), George Brett (228), Jim Rice (616), Gary Carter (620) and Keith Hernandez (623) . . . Don Wilson (455) died after cards went to press (January 5, 1975) . . . Card of Brett lists for $50 . . . Cards of Rice and Carter list for $35 . . . Complete set lists for $475 . . . TOPPS also tested the complete 660-card series in a smaller size (2¼" x 3 1/8") in certain areas of USA in a limited supply . . . Complete set of "Mini-Cards" lists for $700.

1976: As in 1974 there was a 44-card Traded Series . . . Set features five Father & Son cards (66-70) and ten All-Time All-Stars (341-350) . . . Card of Pete Rose (240) lists for $15 . . . Cards of Jim Rice (340), Gary Carter (441) and George Brett (19) list for $12 . . . Complete set lists for $225.

1977: Set features rookie cards of Andre Dawson (473) and Dale Murphy (476) . . . Reuschel Brother Combination (634) shows the two (Paul and Rick) misidentified . . . Dave Collins (431) is photo of Bob Jones . . . Card of Murphy lists for $65 . . . Card of Pete Rose (450) lists for $8.50 . . . Complete set lists for $250.

1978: Record Breakers (1-7) feature Lou Brock, Sparky Lyle, Willie McCovey, Brooks Robinson, Pete Rose, Nolan Ryan and Reggie Jackson . . . Set features rookie cards of Jack Morris (703), Lou Whitaker (704), Paul Molitor/Alan Trammell (707), Lance Parrish (708) and Eddie Murray (36) . . . Card of Murray lists for $35 . . . Card of Parrish lists for $35 . . . Complete set lists for $200.

1979: Bump Wills (369) was originally shown with Blue Jays affiliation but later corrected to Rangers . . . Set features rookie cards of Ozzie Smith (116), Pedro Guerrero (719), Lonnie Smith (722) and Terry Kennedy (724) . . . Larry Cox (489) is photo of Dave Rader . . . Card of Dale Murphy (39) lists for $8 . . . Cards of Ozzie Smith and Eddie Murray (640) list for $7.50 . . . Complete set lists for $135.

1980: Highlights (1-6) feature Hall-of-Famers Lou Brock, Carl Yastrzemski, Willie McCovey and Pete Rose . . . Set features rookie cards of Dave Stieb (77), Rickey Henderson (482) and Dan Quisenberry (667) . . . Card of Henderson lists for $28 . . . Card of Dale Murphy (274) lists for $5.50 . . . Complete set lists for $135.

1981: Set features rookie cards of Fernando Valenzuela (302), Kirk Gibson (315), Harold Baines (347) and Tim Raines (479) . . . Jeff Cox (133) is photo of Steve McCatty . . . John Littlefield (489) is photo of Mark Riggins . . . Card of Valenzuela lists for $7.50 . . . Card of Raines lists for $9 . . . Complete set lists for $80.

1982: Pascual Perez (383) printed with no position on front lists for $35, later corrected . . . Set features rookie cards of Cal Ripken (21), Jesse Barfield (203), Steve Sax (681) and Kent Hrbek (766) . . . Dave Rucker (261) is photo of Roger Weaver . . . Steve Bedrosian (502) is photo of Larry Owen . . . Card of Ripken lists for $12.50 . . . Cards of Barfield and Sax list for $5 . . . Complete set lists for $75.

1983: Record Breakers (1-6) feature Tony Armas, Rickey Henderson, Greg Minton, Lance Parrish, Manny Trillo and John Wathan . . . A series of Super Veterans features early and current photos of 34 leading players . . . Set features rookie cards of Tony Gwynn (482) and Wade Boggs (498) . . . Card of Boggs lists for $32 . . . Card of Gwynn lists for $16 . . . Complete set lists for $85.

1984: Highlights (1-6) salute eleven different players . . . A parade of superstars is included in Active Leaders (701-718) . . . Set features rookie card of Don Mattingly (8) listing for $35 . . . Card of Darryl Strawberry (182) lists for $10 . . . Complete set lists for $85.

1985: A Father & Son Feature (131-143) is again included . . . Set features rookie cards of Scott Bankhead (393), Mike Dunne (395), Shane Mack (398), John Marzano (399), Oddibe McDowell (400), Mark McGwire (401), Pat Pacillo (402), Cory Snyder (403) and Billy Swift (404) as part of salute to 1984 USA Baseball Team (389-404) that participated in Olympic Games plus rookie cards of Roger Clemens (181) and Eric Davis (627) . . . Card of McGwire lists for $20 . . . Card of Davis lists for $18 . . . Card of Clemens lists for $11 . . . Complete set lists for $95.

1986: Set includes Pete Rose Feature (2-7), which reproduces each of Rose's TOPPS cards from 1963 thru 1985 (four per card) . . . Bob Rodgers (141) should have been numbered 171 . . . Ryne Sandberg (690) is the only card with TOPPS logo omitted . . . Complete set lists for $24.

1987: Record Breakers (1-7) feature Roger Clemens, Jim Deshaies, Dwight Evans, Davey Lopes, Dave Righetti, Ruben Sierra and Todd Worrell . . . Jim Gantner (108) is shown with Brewers logo reversed . . . Complete set lists for $22.

1988: Record Breakers (1-7) include Vince Coleman, Don Mattingly, Mark McGwire, Eddie Murray, Phil & Joe Niekro, Nolan Ryan and Benny Santiago. Al Leiter (18) was originally shown with photo of minor leaguer Steve George and later corrected. Complete set lists for $20.00.

Pitching Record & Index

PLAYER	G	IP	W	L	R	ER	SO	BB	GS	CG	SHO	SV	ERA
AGOSTO, JUAN	171	190.1	9	10	104	93	110	86	1	0	0	16	4.40
ANDERSEN, LARRY	289	452	12	15	217	187	251	142	1	0	0	14	3.72
ANDERSON, JOHN	24	45	0	0			19	14	1	0	0	9	6.40
ANDUJAR, JOAQUIN	369	2014	122	108	869	781	965	684	282	67	19	9	3.49
BANNISTER, FLOYD	300	1832.1	101	117	908	820	1405	680	284	49	14	0	4.03
BARLOW, MIKE	133	247	10	6			96	104	2	0	0	6	4.63
BELINSKY, BO	146	665	28	51			476	323	102	14	6	0	4.10
BILLINGHAM, JACK	476	2232	145	113			1141	750	305	74	27	15	3.83
BLASINGAME, WADE	222	864	46	51			512	372	128	16	2	5	4.52
BOONE, DANNY	57	91.2	2	1			55	28	1	0	0	6	3.44
BOUTON, JIM	304	1237	62	63			720	435	144	34	11	6	3.58
BROWN, HAL	358	1680	85	92			733	389	167	47	13	11	3.81
BRUCE, BOB	219	1123	49	71			733	340	171	26	6	1	3.85
BRUNET, GEORGE	324	1431	69	93			921	581	213	39	15	7	3.62
BUZHARDT, JOHN	326	1489	71	96			678	457	200	44	15	7	3.67
CALHOUN, JEFF	73	105.2	3	6	40		72	38	0	0	0	4	2.64
CAPPUZZELLO, GEORGE	35	53.1	1	2		31	32	25	3	0	0	1	3.21
CARDINAL, RANDY	6	13	0	1			7	7	1	0	0	0	6.23
CARPIN, FRANK	49	46	4	1			29	30	0	0	0	4	3.72
CICOTTE, AL	102	260	10	13			149	119	16	1	0	4	4.36
COOK, RON	46	108	4	8			60	50	0	0	0	2	4.00
COOMBS, DANNY	144	393	19	27			249	162	5	2	1	8	4.08
COSGROVE, MIKE	119	275	11	11			122	145	20	2	0	8	4.03
CRAWFORD, JIM	181	431	15	28			276	182	14	1	0	13	4.41
CUELLAR, MIKE	453	2807	185	130			1632	822	379	172	36	11	3.14
CULVER, GEORGE	335	789	48	49			451	352	57	7	2	23	3.62
DARWIN, DANNY	295	1241	72	78	571	490	789	400	141	38	7	17	3.55
DAWLEY, BILL	203	356.1	22	20	123	114	221	122	0	0	0	23	2.88
DESHAIES, JIM	30	154	12	6	67	61	135	66	28	1	1	0	3.56
DICKSON, JIM	109	143	5	3			86	77	1	0	0	3	4.34
DIERKER, LARRY	356	2335	139	123			1493	711	329	106	25	1	3.30
DILAURO, JACK	65	98	2	7			50	35	4	0	0	0	3.66
DIPINO, FRANK	233	333.1	15	29		141	279	143	6	0	0	43	3.81
DIXON, TOM	62	199.2	9	14	162		94	63	24	0	0	1	4.33
DROTT, DICK	176	687	27	46			460	405	101	14	5	0	4.78
DUKES, TOM	161	217	5	16			169	82	0	0	0	13	4.35
EARLEY, ARNOLD	223	381	12	20			310	184	10	1	0	14	4.49
EILERS, DAVE	81	124	8	6			52	29	0	0	0	3	4.43
FARRELL, DICK	590	1704	106	111			1177	468	134	41	5	83	3.45
FORSCH, KEN	512	2108.2	114	112			1034	576	241	70	18	50	3.37
GIBBON, JOE	419	1119	61	65			743	414	127	20	4	32	3.52
GILSON, HAL	15	25	0	2			20	12	0	0	0	0	5.04
GIUSTI, DAVE	668	1718	100	93			1103	570	133	35	9	145	3.60
GLADDING, FRED	450	600	48	34			394	223	1	0	0	109	3.13
GOLDEN, JIM	69	208	9	13			115	76	20	5	1	0	4.54
GRANGER, WAYNE	451	640	35	35			303	201	10	0	0	108	3.14
GREIF, BILL	231	715	31	67			442	287	97	18	5	19	4.42
GRIFFIN, TOM	401	1493.1	77	94			1054	769	191	29	10	1	4.07
GUINN, SKIP	35	37	1	2			40	27	0	0	0	1	5.35
HARDY, LARRY	84	127	9	4			70	56	1	0	0	2	5.24
HARRIS, BUDDY	22	37	1	1			23	16	0	0	0	0	6.32
HARRIS, LUM	151	819	35	63			232	265	91	46	4	4	4.16
HENRY, BILL R.	527	914	46	50			619	296	44	12	2	90	3.26
HOERNER, JOE	493	563	39	34			412	181	0	0	0	99	2.99
JOHNSON, JERRY	365	771	48	51			489	389	39	7	2	41	4.31
JOHNSON, KEN	334	1736	91	106			1042	413	331	50	7	9	3.46
JONES, GORDON	171	379	15	18			232	120	21	4	2	12	4.16
KEMMERER, RUSS	302	1066	43	59			505	389	109	24	7	8	4.47
KENNEDY, CHARLIE	249	960	42	55			411	495	127	48	7	4	3.84
KERFELD, CHARLIE	72	138	15	4	54	47	107	67	6	0	0	7	3.07
KITTLE, HUB					No major league statistics								
KNEPPER, BOB	338	2145.2	114	118	944	819	1206	642	322	73	27	1	3.44
KONIECZNY, DOUG	44	221	7	17			110	111	36	3	1	0	4.93
KROLL, GARY	71	160	6	7			138	91	13	0	0	4	4.22
LACORTE, FRANK	253	490	23	44			372	258	32	0	0	1	5.01
LACOSS, MIKE	281	1179.2	61	67			487	487	163	21	7	26	4.09
LADD, PETE	205	286.2	17	23			209	96	1	0	0	39	4.14
LAMABE, JACK	285	710	33	41			434	238	49	7	3	15	4.25
LARSEN, DON	412	1549	81	91			849	725	171	44	11	23	3.78
LARSON, DAN	78	322.2	10	25			151	140	43	7	3	0	4.41
LATMAN, BARRY	344	1219	59	68			829	489	134	28	10	16	3.91
LEE, DON	244	828	40	44			467	281	97	13	4	11	3.61
LEMASTER, DENNY	357	1788	90	105			1305	600	249	66	14	1	3.58
LEMONGELLO, MARK	89	537	22	38			209	159	74	17	1	1	4.06
LOPEZ, AURELIO	433	872.1	60	35		341	614	355	9	0	0	92	3.52
MACKENZIE, KEN	129	207	8	10			142	63	1	0	0	5	4.83
MADDEN, MIKE	58	154.1	11	8			89	91	20	0	0	0	3.91
MARSHALL, MIKE G.	723	1386	97	112			880	514	24	3	0	187	3.15
MATHIS, RON	23	70	3	5			34	27	8	0	0	0	6.04
MCLAUGHLIN, BO	156	313.1	10	20			188	123	21	0	0	9	4.48
MCMAHON, DON	874	1312	90	68			1003	579	2	0	0	153	2.96
MOFFITT, RANDY	534	782	43	52			455	286	1	0	0	96	3.65
MONTEAGUDO, AURELIO	75	131	3	7			58	62	7	0	0	4	5.08
NAGY, MIKE	87	420	20	13			170	210	62	11	1	0	4.14
NIEKRO, JOE	670	3426	213	190	1506	1331	1656	1191	472	106	29	16	3.50
NIEMANN, RANDY	116	194.2	8	8	107	98	101	75	10	3	2	0	4.53
NOTTEBART, DON	296	922	36	51			525	283	89	16	2	21	3.66
OSINSKI, DAN	324	590	29	28			400	264	21	5	2	18	2.34
OSTEEN, CLAUDE	541	3460	196	195	1438	1251	1612	940	488	140	40	1	3.30
OWENS, JIM	286	886	42	68			516	340	103	21	1	21	4.31
PENTZ, GENE	104	191	8	9			116	108	4	0	0	7	3.63
PIZARRO, JUAN	488	2035	131	105			1520	888	245	79	17	28	3.43
PLADSON, GORDY	20	50.1	0	4			18	23	6	0	0	0	6.08
RAY, JIM	308	618	45	30			407	271	20	1	0	25	3.61
RAYMOND, CLAUDE	449	720	46	53			497	225	7	2	0	83	3.66
REED, HOWIE	229	516	26	29			268	208	35	3	1	9	3.72
REUSS, JERRY	537	3218.2	194	163			1744	1018	468	123	37	11	3.50
RICCELLI, FRANK	17	41	3	3			32	23	5	0	0	0	4.39
RICHARD, J.R.	238	1606	107	71			1491	770	221	76	19	0	3.15
ROBERGE, BERT	125	190.1	12	8			99	70	0	0	0	9	3.64
ROBERTS, DAVE A.	445	2098	103	125			957	615	277	77	20	15	3.78
ROBERTS, ROBIN	676	4689	286	245			2357	902	609	305	45	25	3.40
RUHLE, VERN	327	1410.1	67	88			582	348	188	29	12	1	3.73
RYAN, NOLAN	611	4115.1	253	226	1643	1440	4277	2268	577	203	54	3	3.15
SAMBITO, JOE	414	590.2	35	32	212	183	454	179	1	0	0	84	2.79
SCHERMAN, FRED	346	537	33	26			297	245	8	1	0	39	3.84
SCHNEIDER, DAN	117	166	9	7			86	70	8	0	0	4	4.72
SCOTT, MIKE	212	1160	65	62			750	363	185	16	10	0	3.70
SEMBERA, CARROLL	99	140	3	11			94	73	1	0	0	6	4.69
SHANTZ, BOBBY	537	1936	119	99	541	477	1072	643	171	78	15	48	3.38

PLAYER	G	IP	W	L	R	ER	SO	BB	GS	CG	SHO	SV	ERA
SHEA, STEVE	40	51	4	4			26	19	0	0	0	6	3.18
SIEBERT, PAUL	87	129	3	8			59	73	7	1	1	3	3.77
SMITH, BILLY L.	10	21	1	1			3	3	1	0	0	1	3.00
SMITH, DAVE	361	526.2	38	29	177	153	337	181	1	0	0	100	2.61
SOLANO, JULIO	35	56.2	1	5			36	22	0	0	0	0	2.38
SOSA, JOSE	34	59	1	3			36	29	2	0	0	1	4.58
SPINKS, SCIPIO	35	202	7	12			154	107	29	7	0	0	3.75
SPROWL, BOBBY	22	47	0	3			34	27	4	0	0	0	5.36
STANTON, MIKE	242	343.1	12	19			275	153	3	0	0	30	4.40
STONE, DEAN	215	687	29	39			380	373	85	19	5	12	4.47
SUTTON, DON	7235	5002.2	310	239	1959	1776	3431	1272	706	177	58	5	3.20
TAYLOR, RON	491	799	45	43			464	209	17	3	0	72	3.93
THOMAS, ROY	174	398	19	11			275	185	13	0	0	7	3.75
THROOP, GEORGE	30	42	2	0			27	35	0	0	0	3	3.86
TIEFENAUER, BOB	179	316	9	25			204	87	7	0	0	23	3.84
UMBRICHT, JIM	88	194	9	5			133	71	7	0	0	3	3.06
UPSHAW, CECIL	348	563	34	36			323	177	0	0	0	86	3.13
VON HOFF, BRUCE	13	53	0	3			23	30	10	0	0	0	5.09
WARTHEN, DAN	83	308	12	3			224	198	41	5	1	3	4.30
WATKINS, BOB	5	16	0	0			11	13	0	0	0	0	5.06
WILLIAMS, RICK	48	156	5	9			54	40	17	2	2	0	3.58
WILLIS, RON	188	239	11	12			128	119	0	0	0	19	3.31
WILSON, DON	270	1748	104	92			1283	640	245	78	20	2	3.15
WITT, GEORGE	66	229	11	16			156	127	38	5	3	0	4.32
WOMACK, DOOLEY	193	302	19	18			177	111	1	0	0	24	2.95
WOODESHICK, HAL	427	847	44	62			484	389	62	7	1	61	3.56
YELLEN, LARRY	14	26	0	0			12	11	2	0	0	0	6.23
YORK, JIM	174	285	16	17			194	132	4	0	0	10	3.79
ZACHARY, CHRIS	108	321	10	29			184	122	40	1	1	2	4.51
ZAMORA, OSCAR	158	225	13	15			99	60	2	0	0	23	7.16

Batting Record & Index

PLAYER	G	AB	R	H	2B	3B	HR	RBI	SB	SLG	BB	SO	AVG
ADLESH, DAVE	106	256	9	43	3	1	1	11	0	.199	18	80	.168
AGEE, TOMMIE	1129	3912	558	999	170	27	130	433	167	.412	342	918	.255
ALOU, JESUS	1380	4345	448	1216	170	26	32	377	31	.353	138	267	.280
AMALFITANO, JOE	643	1715	248	418	67	19	9	123	19	.321	185	224	.244
ANDREWS, ROB	493	1454	154	365	30	15	3	91	33	.298	148	121	.251
ASHBY, ALAN	1150	3449	321	835	156	12	69	414	7	.354	375	525	.242
ASPROMONTE, BOB	1324	4369	386	1103	135	26	60	457	19	.336	333	459	.252
BAILEY, MARK	279	829	94	188	35	1	23	94	1	.355	148	186	.227
BALDWIN, REGGIE	52	87	5	21	6	0	0	12	0	.345	4	12	.241
BALES, WES	31	43	8	4	0	0	0	2	0	.093	8	12	.093
BANNISTER, ALAN	972	3007	430	811	143	28	19	288	108	.355	292	319	.270
BASS, KEVIN	546	1689	219	462	84	18	40	195	48	.416	82	228	.274
BATEMAN, JOHN	1017	3330	250	765	123	8	81	375	10	.350	172	610	.230
BEAUCHAMP, JIM	393	661	79	153	18	4	14	90	6	.334	54	150	.231
BERGMAN, DAVE	1537	1253	151	310	43	10	26	130	12	.360	179	170	.247
BERRA, DALE	792	2400	223	570	99	18	47	263	32	.345	193	396	.238
BIANCALANA, BUDDY	256	479	65	102	15	7	5	23	8	.305	39	135	.213
BJORKMAN, GEORGE	29	75	8	17	4	0	2	14	0	.360	16	29	.227
BLEFARY, CURT	863	2489	340	583	78	15	101	324	16	.399	456	444	.234
BOCHY, BRUCE	320	727	67	180	34	1	24	82	1	.399	56	156	.248
BOND, WALT	365	1199	149	307	40	11	41	179	10	.410	106	175	.256
BOSWELL, KEN	930	2517	266	625	91	19	31	234	27	.337	260	259	.248
BRAND, RON	568	1345	108	322	34	7	3	106	20	.282	112	126	.239
BRANDT, JACKIE	1221	3895	540	1020	175	37	112	485	45	.412	351	574	.262
BROWN, OLLIE	1221	3642	404	964	144	11	111	454	40	.402	314	616	.265
BROWNE, BYRON	349	869	94	205	37	10	32	102	5	.405	101	273	.236
BRUMMER, GLENN	178	347	23	87	16	0	1	27	4	.305	25	54	.251
BRYANT, DON	59	109	6	24	3	0	1	13	1	.275	6	25	.220
BUDDIN, DON	711	2289	342	551	123	12	41	225	15	.359	404	404	.241
BUSBY, JIM	1352	4250	541	1113	162	35	48	438	97	.350	310	439	.262
BUSSE, RAY	68	155	12	23	8	2	2	9	0	.265	11	54	.148
CABELL, ENOS	1688	5952	753	1647	263	56	60	596	238	.370	259	691	.277
CAMPBELL, DAVE	428	1252	128	267	52	4	20	89	29	.311	102	254	.213
CAMPBELL, JIM	82	244	15	54	7	0	7	25	0	.336	16	63	.221
CANNON, JOE	148	227	34	40	3	1	0	11	6	.211	15	54	.176
CEDENO, CESAR	1969	7232	1079	2069	434	59	199	970	549	.445	657	925	.286
CERV, BOB	829	2261	320	624	96	26	105	374	12	.481	212	392	.276
CHILES, RICH	284	618	68	157	37	2	6	76	2	.350	65	65	.254
COLBERT, NATE	1004	3422	481	833	141	25	173	520	52	.451	383	902	.243
CRAWFORD, WILLIE	1210	3435	507	921	152	35	86	419	47	.408	431	664	.268
CRUZ, JOSE	2189	7472	980	2147	372	90	153	1032	313	.423	854	958	.278
DAVANON, JERRY	262	499	73	117	21	2	3	50	3	.315	68	80	.234
DAVIS, BROCK	243	543	46	141	12	4	1	43	7	.306	57	73	.260
DAVIS, GLENN	276	985	148	260	48	4	54	173	3	.483	95	152	.264
DAVIS, RON E.	295	853	96	199	44	6	10	79	9	.334	56	160	.233
DAVIS, TOMMY	1999	7223	811	2121	272	35	153	1052	136	.405	381	754	.294
DORAN, BILL	620	2308	349	633	93	27	32	182	103	.380	308	273	.274
DRIESSEN, DAN	1196	3703	734	1440	277	23	151	749	154	.412	745	705	.268
DRUMRIGHT, KEITH	48	141	13	34	1	1	0	13	1	.262	7	8	.241
DUROCHER, LEO	1637	5379	575	1320	210	56	24	567	31	.320	377	480	.247
EASLER, MIKE	1053	3400	445	1000	179	25	113	491	19	.461	301	644	.294
EDWARDS, JOHNNY	1470	4577	430	1106	202	32	81	524	15	.353	465	635	.242
FENWICK, BOB	41	56	7	10	2	0	0	1	0	.232	3	5	.179
FERGUSON, JOE	1013	2951	407	719	121	8	122	445	24	.413	565	607	.244
FISCHLIN, MIKE	516	941	109	207	29	6	3	68	22	.273	92	142	.220
FOX, NELLIE	2367	9232	1279	2663	355	112	35	790	76	.363	719	216	.288

PLAYER	G	AB	R	H	2B	3B	HR	RBI	SB	SLG	BB	SO	AVG
FREESE, GENE	1115	3446	429	877	161	28	115	432	51	.418	243	535	.254
FULLER, JIM	107	315	24	61	17	0	11	41	0	.352	19	130	.194
GAINES, JOE	362	771	104	186	25	9	21	95	14	.379	81	197	.241
GALLAGHER, BOB	213	255	34	56	6	1	2	13	1	.275	16	56	.220
GARNER, PHIL	1732	5885	751	1543	290	82	104	714	219	.392	535	795	.262
GEIGER, GARY	954	2569	388	633	91	29	77	283	62	.394	341	466	.246
GENTILE, JIM	936	2922	434	759	113	6	179	549	3	.486	475	663	.260
GERNERT, DICK	835	2493	357	632	104	8	103	402	10	.426	363	462	.254
GERONIMO, CESAR	1522	3780	460	977	161	50	51	392	82	.368	354	746	.258
GOMEZ, PRESTON	8	7	2	2	1	0	0	2	0	.429	0	4	.286
GONZALEZ, JULIO	370	969	90	228	32	8	4	66	13	.297	36	132	.235
GOODMAN, BILLY	1623	5644	807	1691	299	44	19	591	37	.378	669	329	.300
GOSS, HOWIE	222	522	56	113	24	3	15	54	4	.333	40	164	.216
GOTAY, JULIO	389	988	106	257	38	5	6	70	12	.323	61	127	.260
GROSS, GREG	1537	3404	423	993	125	45	6	287	39	.360	471	399	.292
GROTE, JERRY	1421	4339	352	1092	160	22	39	404	15	.326	399	600	.252
HARDY, CARROLL	433	1117	172	251	47	10	17	113	8	.330	120	222	.225
HARRIS, ALONZO	6	1	0	0	0	0	0	0	0	.000	0	1	.000
HARRISON, CHUCK	328	1012	94	241	43	6	17	126	3	.343	85	147	.238
HARTMAN, J.C.	90	238	13	44	6	0	0	8	2	.210	6	29	.185
HATCHER, BILLY	188	591	80	149	27	4	5	46	42	.355	31	64	.252
HATTON, GRADY	1312	4206	562	1068	166	33	91	533	42	.374	646	430	.254
HEATH, BILL	112	199	13	47	6	1	1	13	1	.276	26	22	.236
HEEP, DANNY	560	1313	144	338	71	6	25	149	6	.376	153	175	.257
HEIST, AL	177	495	63	126	20	8	6	46	6	.368	52	72	.255
HELMS, TOMMY	1435	4997	414	1342	223	21	34	477	33	.342	231	301	.269
HERRERA, JOSE	80	231	16	61	10	0	2	20	1	.333	7	28	.264
HERRMANN, ED	922	2729	247	654	92	4	80	320	6	.364	260	361	.240
HERTZ, STEVE	5	4	2	0	0	0	0	0	0	.000	0	3	.000
HIATT, JACK	483	1142	110	287	51	5	28	154	0	.363	224	295	.251
HOUSEHOLDER, PAUL	426	1236	140	295	56	10	28	127	35	.368	115	232	.239
HOWARD, LARRY	133	365	36	86	19	1	6	47	0	.337	37	85	.236
HOWARD, WILBUR	466	1081	108	267	37	11	6	71	56	.322	45	175	.250
HOWE, ART	887	2623	268	682	139	23	43	293	10	.380	275	287	.260
IVIE, MIKE	857	2694	309	724	133	17	81	411	22	.421	214	402	.269
JACKSON, SONNY	936	3055	396	767	81	28	7	162	126	.303	250	265	.251
JOHNSON, CLIFF	1369	3945	539	1016	198	10	196	699	13	.462	568	719	.258
JUTZE, SKIP	254	656	45	141	14	3	3	51	5	.259	34	86	.215
KASKO, EDDIE	1077	3546	411	935	146	33	22	261	31	.331	265	353	.264
KELLEHER, MICK	622	1081	108	230	32	6	0	65	9	.253	74	133	.213
KING, HAL	322	683	67	146	26	0	24	82	1	.366	104	158	.214
KNICELY, ALAN	194	439	40	95	14	0	11	55	0	.323	51	107	.216
KNIGHT, RAY	1240	3967	410	1102	230	25	67	497	13	.399	284	459	.278
LAMPARD, KEITH	62	84	10	20	8	1	1	7	0	.393	5	27	.238
LANDESTOY, RAFAEL	596	1230	134	291	32	17	4	83	54	.300	100	123	.237
LANDIS, JIM	1346	4288	625	1061	169	50	93	467	139	.375	588	767	.247
LANIER, HAL	1196	3703	297	843	111	20	8	273	11	.275	136	436	.228
LARKER, NORM	667	1953	227	538	97	15	32	271	3	.390	211	165	.275
LEONARD, JEFFREY	862	2964	379	808	127	31	81	428	120	.418	221	618	.273
LILLIS, BOB	817	2328	198	549	68	9	3	137	23	.277	99	116	.236
LOPES, DAVE	1765	6311	1019	1661	230	50	154	608	555	.389	820	844	.263
MAHONEY, JIM	120	210	32	48	4	1	4	15	1	.314	11	47	.229
MANTILLA, FELIX	969	2707	360	707	97	10	89	330	27	.403	256	352	.261
MARTINEZ, MARTY	436	945	97	230	19	11	0	57	7	.287	70	107	.243
MATHEWS, EDDIE	2391	8537	1509	2315	354	72	512	1453	68	.509	1444	1487	.271
MAY, LEE	2071	7609	959	2031	340	31	354	1244	39	.459	487	1570	.267

PLAYER	G	AB	R	H	2B	3B	HR	RBI	SB	SLG	BB	SO	AVG
MAY, MILT	1192	3693	313	971	147	11	77	443	4	.371	305	361	.265
MAYBERRY, JOHN	1620	5447	733	1379	211	19	255	879	20	.439	881	810	.253
MAYE, LEE	1288	4048	533	1109	190	39	94	419	59	.410	282	481	.274
MCCLURE, JACK						No major league statistics							
MCFADDEN, LEON	62	121	5	26	3	0	0	4	2	.240	10	19	.215
MEJIAS, ROMAN	627	1768	212	449	57	12	54	202	20	.391	89	238	.254
MENKE, DENIS	1598	5071	605	1270	225	40	101	606	34	.370	698	853	.250
METZGER, ROGER	1219	4201	453	972	101	71	5	254	41	.317	355	449	.231
MILBOURNE, LARRY	989	2448	290	623	71	24	11	184	133	.321	133	176	.254
MILLER, NORM	540	1364	166	325	68	10	24	159	16	.356	160	265	.238
MIZEROCK, JOHN	92	204	23	37	9	2	0	22	0	.275	38	39	.181
MORENO, OMAR	1382	4992	699	1257	171	87	37	386	487	.343	387	885	.252
MORGAN, JOE L.	2650	9281	1651	2518	449	96	268	1143	689	.427	1865	1015	.271
MUMPHREY, JERRY	1404	4618	616	1330	196	53	57	522	173	.390	436	625	.288
MURRELL, IVAN	564	1306	126	308	41	15	33	123	20	.366	44	342	.236
NICHOLSON, DAVE	538	1419	184	301	32	12	61	179	6	.381	219	573	.212
PANKOVITS, JIM	198	366	42	97	16	1	6	35	4	.363	30	74	.265
PARKER, SALTY	11	25	6	7	2	0	0	4	0	.360	2	3	.280
PENDLETON, JIM	444	941	120	240	30	8	19	97	11	.365	43	151	.255
PEPITONE, JOE	1397	5097	606	1315	158	35	219	721	41	.432	302	526	.258
PETERS, FRANK						No major league statistics							
PISKER, DON						No major league statistics							
PITTMAN, JOE	139	285	29	75	7	2	0	16	13	.302	20	37	.263
POINTER, AARON	40	101	11	21	5	0	2	15	2	.317	18	33	.208
PUHL, TERRY	1155	4086	579	1150	188	50	57	363	184	.394	406	413	.281
PUJOLS, LUIS	315	849	50	163	27	6	6	81	1	.259	52	164	.192
RADER, DOUG	1465	5186	631	1302	245	39	155	722	37	.403	528	1057	.251
RANEW, MERRITT	269	594	68	147	20	9	8	54	2	.352	42	120	.247
REYNOLDS, CRAIG	1177	3742	409	968	115	62	35	321	49	.351	170	321	.259
REYNOLDS, RONN	97	239	16	49	7	0	3	13	0	.272	14	61	.205
RICHARDT, MIKE	186	580	46	131	15	1	4	60	11	.276	27	62	.226
RIVERA, GERMAN	107	244	21	65	13	2	2	17	1	.361	23	32	.266
ROBERTS, DAVE L.	91	194	15	38	8	1	2	17	0	.278	22	43	.196
ROBERTS, DAVE W.	709	2017	194	483	77	7	49	208	27	.353	128	361	.239
ROBERTS, LEON	901	2737	342	731	126	28	78	328	26	.419	256	428	.267
RUNNELS, PETE	1799	6373	876	1854	282	64	49	630	37	.378	844	627	.291
SCOTT, TONY	991	2803	331	699	111	28	17	253	125	.327	186	464	.249
SEXTON, JIMMY	236	372	53	81	9	2	5	24	36	.298	32	71	.218
SIMPSON, DICK	288	518	94	107	19	2	15	56	10	.338	64	174	.207
SIMS, GREG	7	6	1	1	0	0	0	0	0	.167	1	3	.167
SMITH, HAL W.	879	2682	269	715	148	10	58	323	7	.394	196	361	.267
SPANGLER, AL	912	2267	307	594	87	26	21	175	37	.351	295	234	.262
SPERRING, ROB	208	473	48	100	13	1	1	30	1	.262	46	107	.211
SPILMAN, HARRY	401	639	80	151	25	0	16	97	0	.351	61	95	.236
STAUB, RUSTY	2951	9720	1189	2716	499	47	292	1466	47	.431	1255	888	.279
STEWART, JIMMY	777	1420	164	336	45	14	8	112	38	.305	139	218	.237
STINSON, BOB	652	1634	166	408	61	7	33	180	8	.356	201	254	.250
SUTHERLAND, GARY	1031	3104	308	754	109	10	24	239	11	.308	207	219	.243
TAUSSIG, DON	153	263	38	69	14	5	2	30	2	.399	21	53	.262
TAVERAS, ALEX	35	53	6	11	1	0	0	4	0	.226	2	3	.208
TEMPLE, JOHNNY	1420	5218	720	1484	208	36	22	395	140	.351	648	338	.284
THOMAS, DERREL	1597	4677	585	1163	154	54	43	370	140	.332	446	593	.249
THOMAS, FRANK	1766	6285	792	1671	262	31	286	962	15	.454	484	894	.266
THOMAS, LEE	1027	3324	405	847	111	22	106	428	25	.397	332	397	.255
THON, DICKIE	649	2079	258	565	99	24	32	192	98	.389	162	275	.272
TOLMAN, TIM	107	150	14	26	8	0	5	21	1	.327	14	25	.173
TORRES, HECTOR	622	1738	148	375	46	7	17	115	7	.281	104	229	.216
TRIANDOS, GUS	1206	3907	389	954	147	6	167	608	1	.413	440	636	.244
VALDESPINO, SANDY	382	765	96	176	23	3	7	67	14	.295	57	129	.230
VIRDON, BILL	1583	5980	735	1596	237	81	91	502	47	.379	442	647	.267

PLAYER	G	AB	R	H	2B	3B	HR	RBI	SB	SLG	BB	SO	AVG
WALKER, HARRY	807	2651	385	786	126	37	10	214	42	.383	245	175	.296
WALKER, TONY	84	90	19	20	7	0	2	10	11	.367	11	15	.222
WALLER, TY	52	104	17	25	2	1	3	14	2	.385	7	28	.240
WALLING, DENNY	903	2133	287	594	95	24	41	294	37	.403	227	219	.278
WALTON, DANNY	297	779	69	174	27	1	28	107	4	.376	88	240	.223
WARWICK, CARL	530	1462	168	363	51	10	31	149	13	.360	127	241	.248
WATSON, BOB	1832	6185	802	1826	307	41	184	989	27	.447	653	796	.295
WEEKLY, JOHNNY	53	121	7	25	4	0	5	19	0	.364	15	21	.207
WHITE, MIKE	100	296	30	78	11	3	0	27	1	.321	21	49	.264
WILLIAMS, GEORGE	59	135	15	31	7	0	0	5	0	.281	10	17	.230
WILLIAMS, WALT	842	2373	284	640	106	11	33	173	34	.365	126	211	.270
WOODS, GARY	525	1032	117	251	50	2	13	110	19	.337	86	187	.243
WYNN, JIM	1920	6653	1105	1665	285	39	291	964	225	.436	1224	1427	.250